BABY BOOM

YUICHI

N PRESS

YOKOYAMA

BREAKDOW

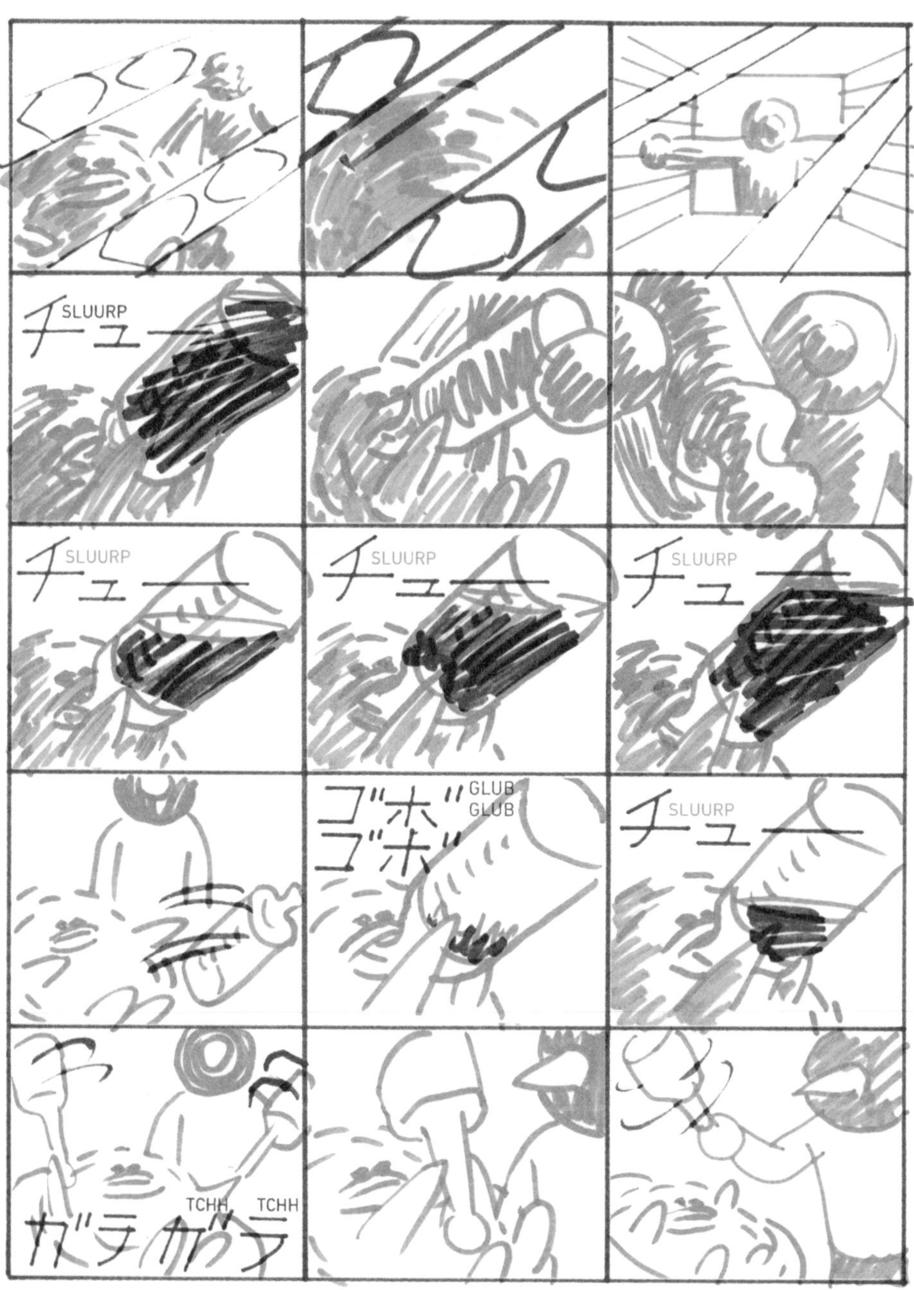
チュー
SLUURP
チュー
SLUURP
チュー
SLUURP
チュー
SLUURP
ゴボゴボ
GLUB GLUB
チュー
SLUURP
ガラガラ
TCHH TCHH

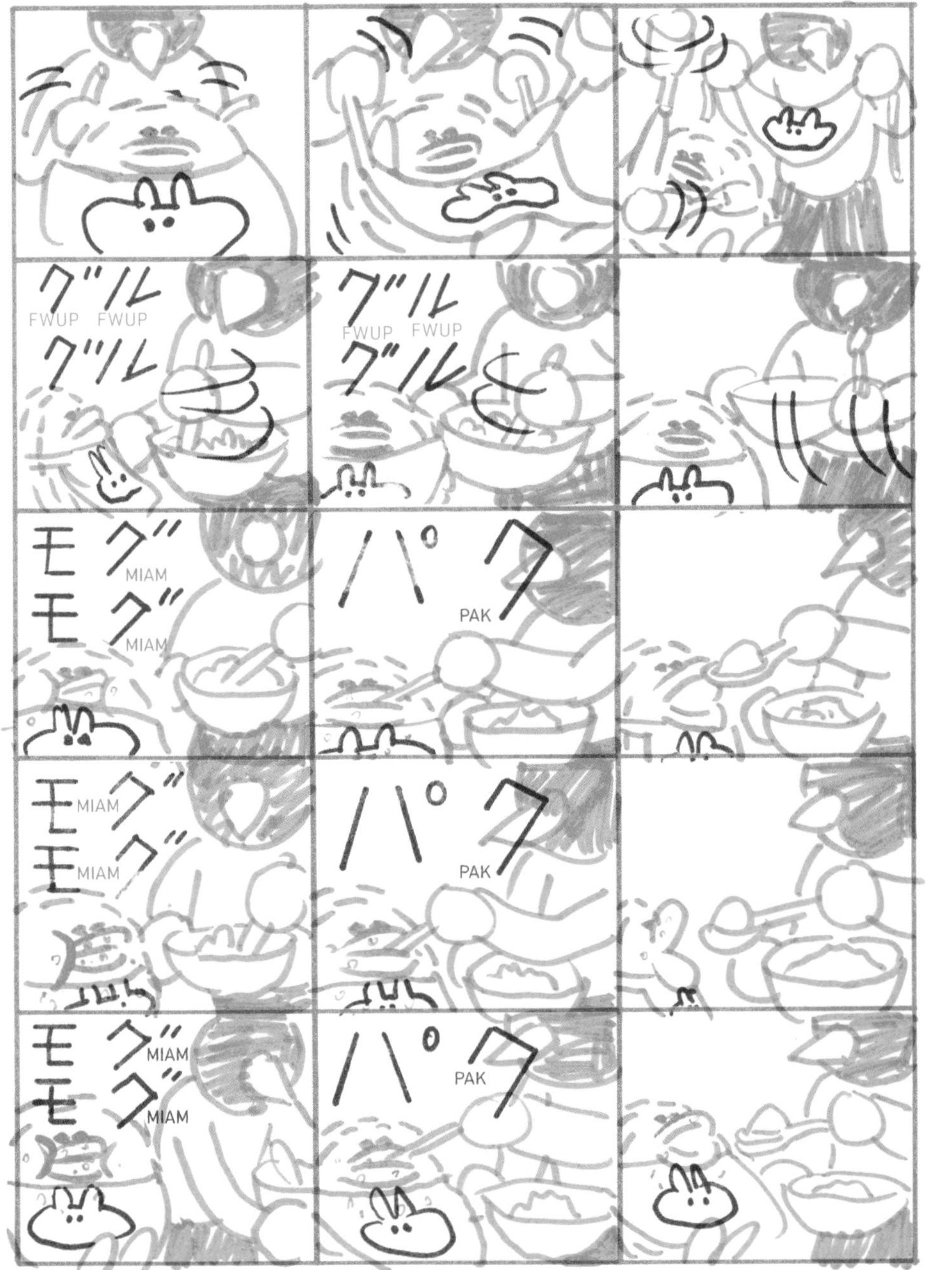

グル
FWUP FWUP
グル
グル
FWUP FWUP
グル
モグ
MIAM
モグ
MIAM
パク
PAK
モグ
MIAM
モグ
MIAM
パク
PAK
モグ
MIAM
モグ
MIAM
パク
PAK

ドスッ
POF
ガラガラ
BRRR
BRRR
KCHUK
BRRR
BRRR
BRRR
BRRR
ガラガラガラガラ
BRRR
BRRR
BRRR
BRRR
BRRR
BRRR

BAM
BRRRRR
PLAC
PLAC
SPLASH
ZBLOOSH
ZBLOOSH
POF
SPLASH
SUD
SUD
SCRUB
SCRUB
SUD
SUD

SPLOOP
CLAP
SCRUB SCRUB
SUD
SUD
SUD
SUD
SPLASH
ZBLOOSH
SCRUB SCRUB
ZBLOOSH
SPLASH
ZBLOOSH

バン
BAM
ガラガラ
TUKA TUKA
ドス
POF
ドス
POF

ドス
POF
ドス
POF
ドス
POF
ドス
POF

ドス
POF
ドス
POF
ガラ
TUKA
TUKA
ガラ

BAP
BAP

SPLOSH
SPLOSH
SPLISH
SPLISH
FSCHHH
FSCHHH
SPLISH SPLISH
SPLISH SPLISH
BOING
FSCHHH
BOING
PLAF
NWOOP
NWOOP

ブーーン VWOOM
ブーーン VWOOM
ズルズル ズルズル SLL SLL
ズルズル
ズルズル SLL SLL
ズルズル SLL SLL
パパパパ PLIP PLIP PLIP PLIP

ドブン SPLOOSH
ドブン SPLOOSH
ザザ FSCH ザザ FSCH ザザ FSCH ザ
バシャ SPLISH
バシャ SPLISH
バシャ SPLISH
バシャ SPLISH
ズルズル SLL SLL
バタ FLAP バタ FLAP バタ FLAP
バタ FLAP バタ FLAP

CLANG
CLING
ガチャガチャ
CLANG
CLING
ガチャガチャ
KTUNK
KTUNK
ガタガタ

バタバタ
FLA FLA
バタ
バタバタ
FLA FLA
バタバタ
バタ
FLA
バタ
FLA

バタ
FLA
バタ
FLA
バタ
FLA
バタ
FLA
バタ
FLA
バタバタバタ
FLA FLA FLA

モクモクモク
PUF
PUF
PUF
ゴォオオオオ
GOOOOO
ブルルルル
VROOOOO
カチ
CLIC
ゴォオオ
GOOOOO
ゴォオオオ
GOOOOO

FSCHH
バサ
FSCHH
バサ
FSCHH
バサ
FSCHH
バサ
バサバサ
FSCHH FSCHH
ガラガラ
KLA KLA
バッ
FLAH

ドス
POF
キュ
SQUIK
BLUB BLUB
FSCHHH
TAP TAP TAP
ZBLOOSH

SQUIB SQUIB
SCHWONK
SQUIB SQUIB
SCHWONK
SQUIB SQUIB

キュ
SQUIIIK
PLOTCH
キュ
SQUIIIK
キュ
SQUIIIK
SCHWONK
キュ
SQUIIIK

BOM
ブラ
SQUIB SQUIB
ブラ
SLU SLU
キュ
SQUIIIK
キュ
SQUIIIK
シャ
SCHWONK
ブラ ブラ
SQUIB SQUIB

SLU SLU SLU SLU
SLU SLU
TAP TAP TAP
SLU SLU SLU
TAP TAP
SLU SLU
SLU SLU SLU
TAP TAP TAP

SLU
SLU
TAP
TAP
TAP
TAP
TAP
TAP
TAP
TAP
TAP
TAP
TAP
TAP
FLIP

ツル
SLU
ツル
SLU
クル
FLIP
ドドド
TAP
TAP
TAP
ドドド
TAP
TAP
TAP
ドバ
ZBLOOSH
ギャ
SCHWONK

ドス
POF
TAP
TAP
TAP
ゴロ
ゴロ
BLOM
BLOM
TAP
TAP
ベターン
FLAC

ガタ
KTUNK
ガタ
KTUNK
ガタ
KTUNK
ガタ
KTUNK
バッ
FLAC
バサ
FFLLL

ドドド
TAP TAP TAP
ドス
POF
ズボ
SPLUSH
ザー
FSCHH
ブチ
POINK
ドス
POF
ドドド
TAP TAP TAP

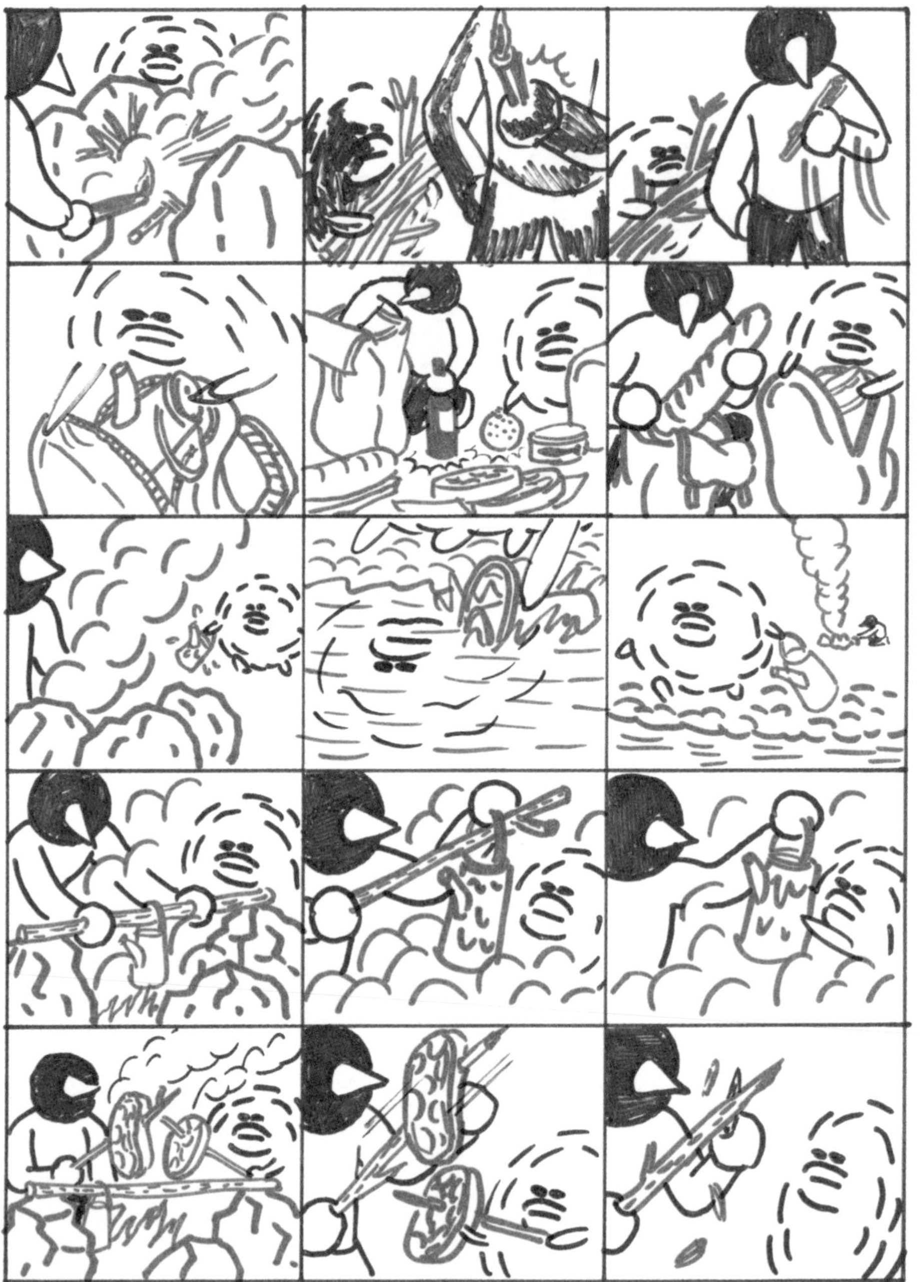

グルグル
FLUP
FLUP
グルグル
FLUP
FLUP
グルグル
FLUP
FLUP
グルグル
FLUP
FLUP
グルグルグル
FLUP
FLUP
FLUP
グイ
GWEEEN

FLUP
FLUP
FLUP
FLUP
FLUP
FLUP
FLUP
FLUP
FLUP
FLUP
FLUP
FLUP
FLUP
FLUP
FLUP
GWEEEN

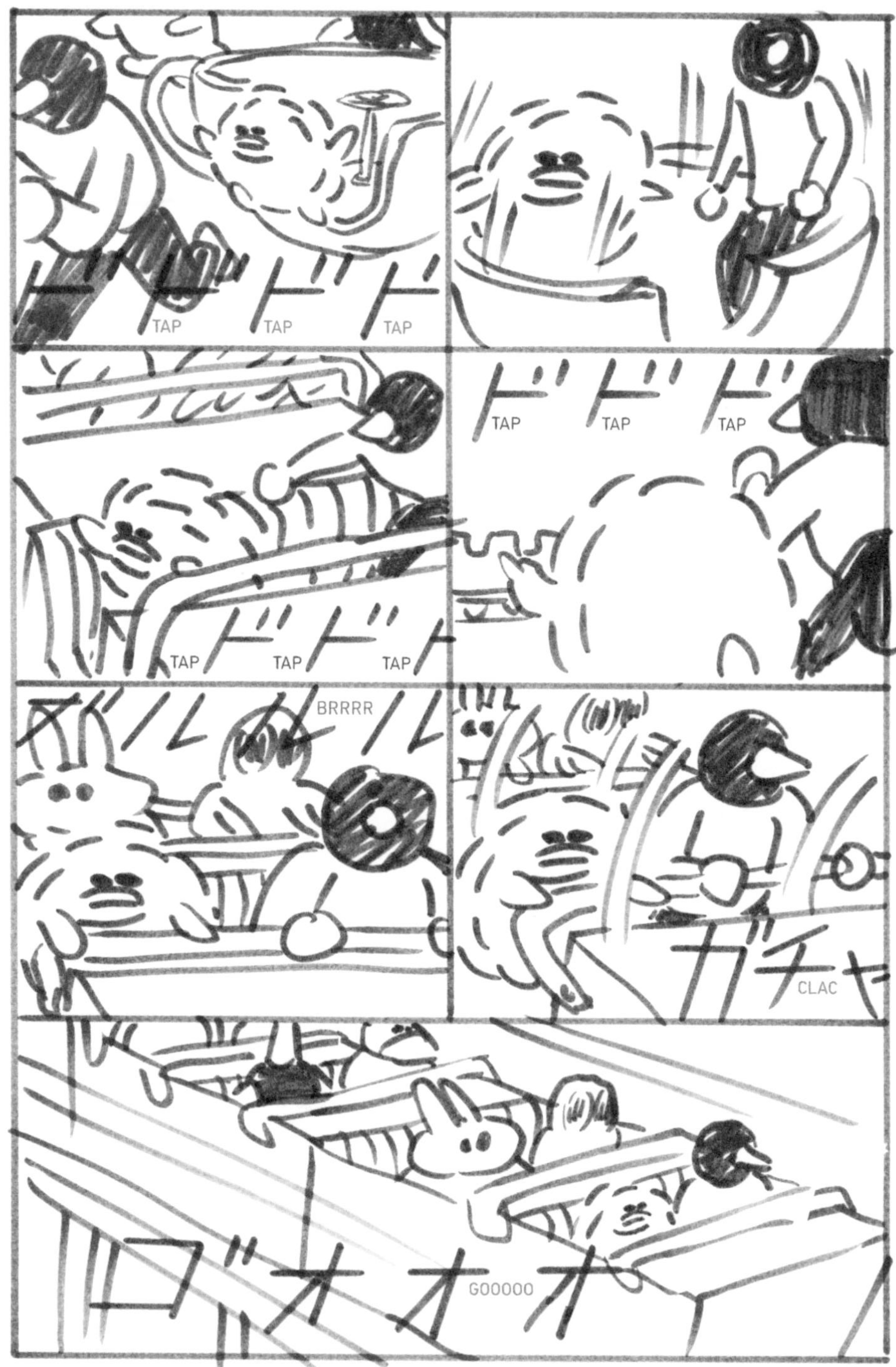

ドドド
TAP TAP TAP
ドドド
TAP TAP TAP
ドドド
TAP TAP TAP
BRRRR
ガチャ
CLAC
ゴオオオ
GOOOOO

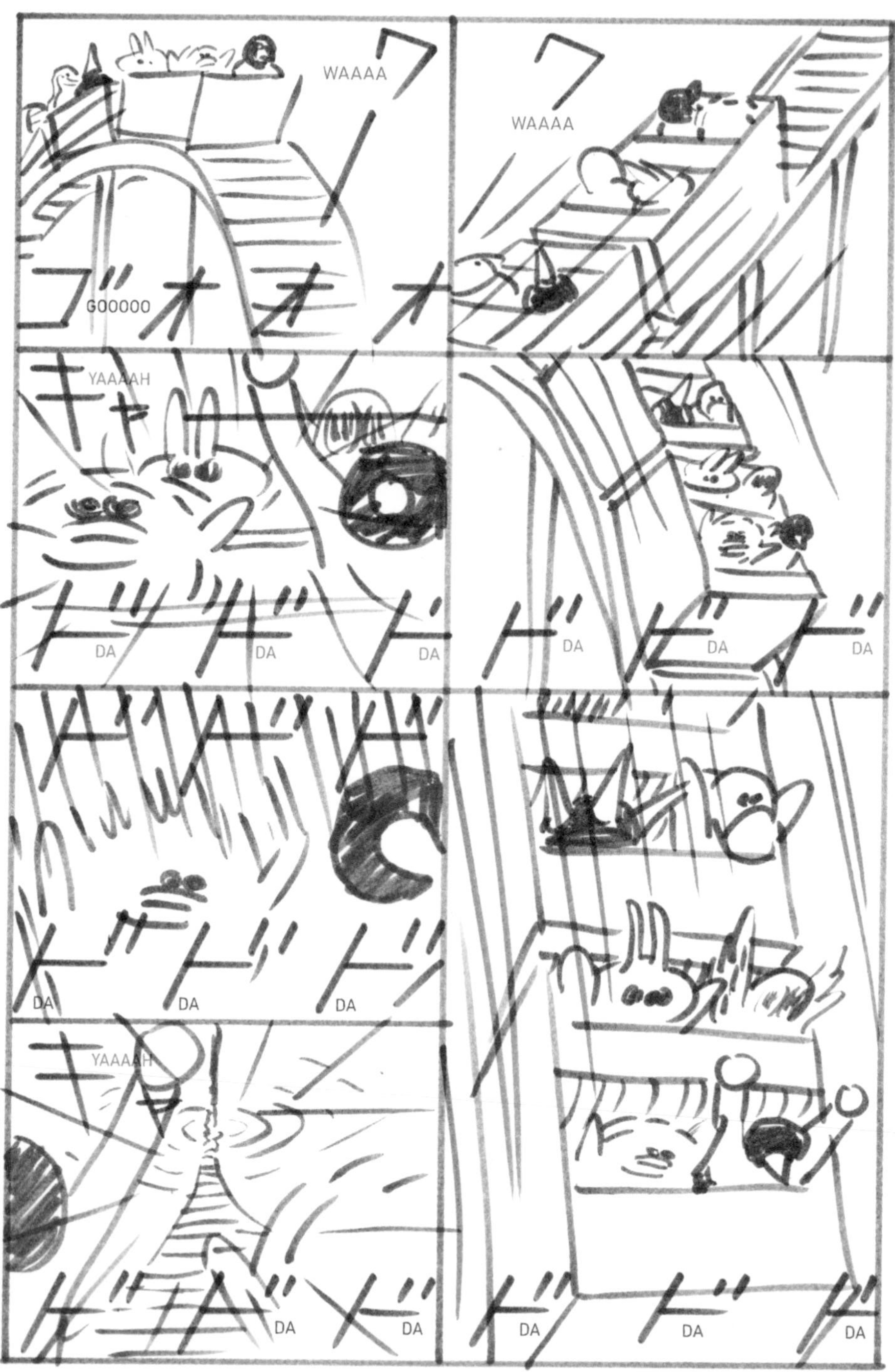
WAAAA
WAAAA
GOOOOO
DA
DA
DA
YAAAAH
DA
DA
DA
DA
DA
DA
DA
DA
YAAAAH
DA
DA

SPLOOSH
FSCHHH
FSCHHH
DA DA DA
YAAAAH
DA DA DA DA
KLA KLA
KLA KLA
KLA KLA
YAAAAH

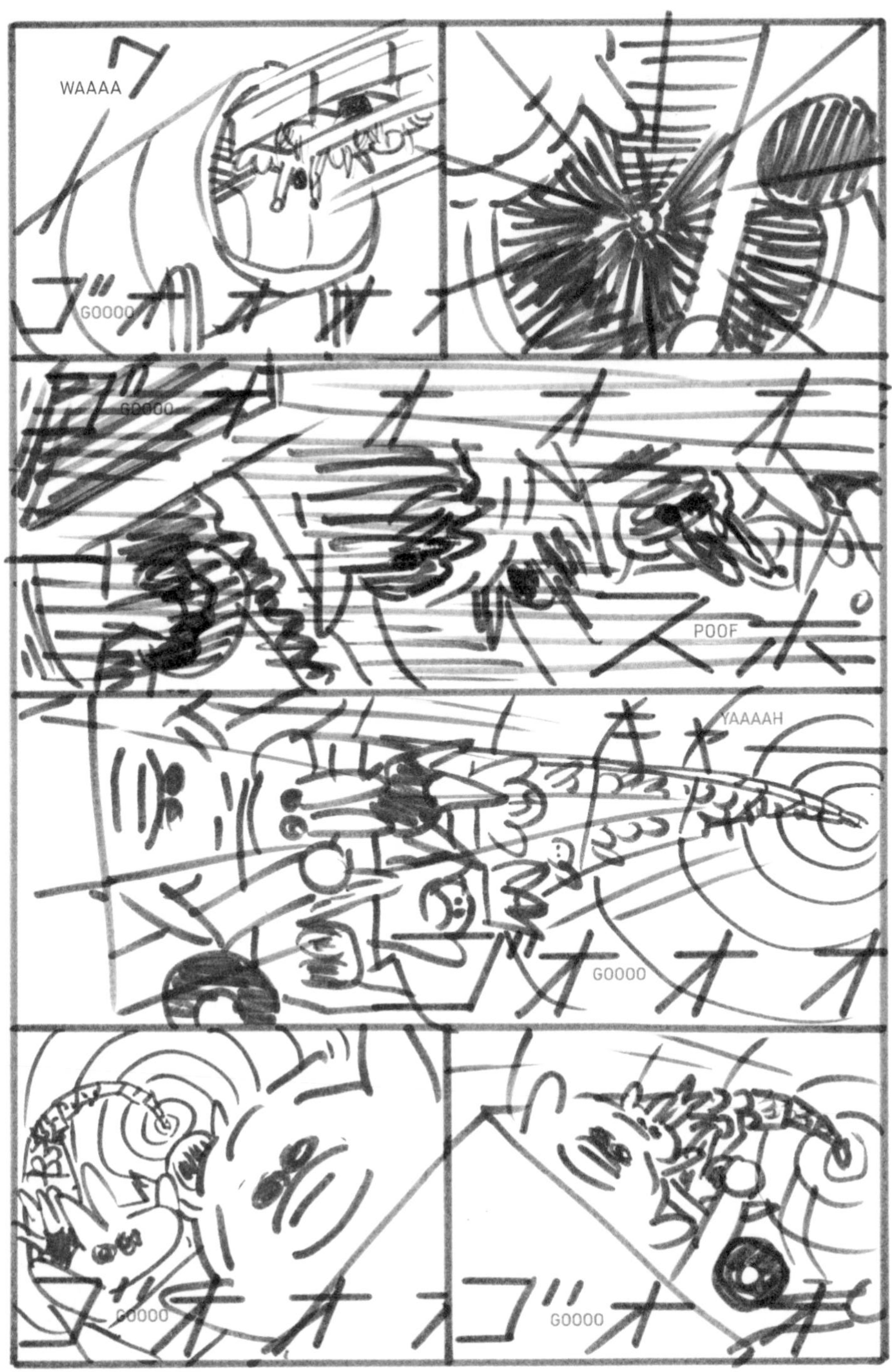
WAAAA
GOOOO
GOOOO
POOF
YAAAAH
GOOOO
GOOOO
GOOOO

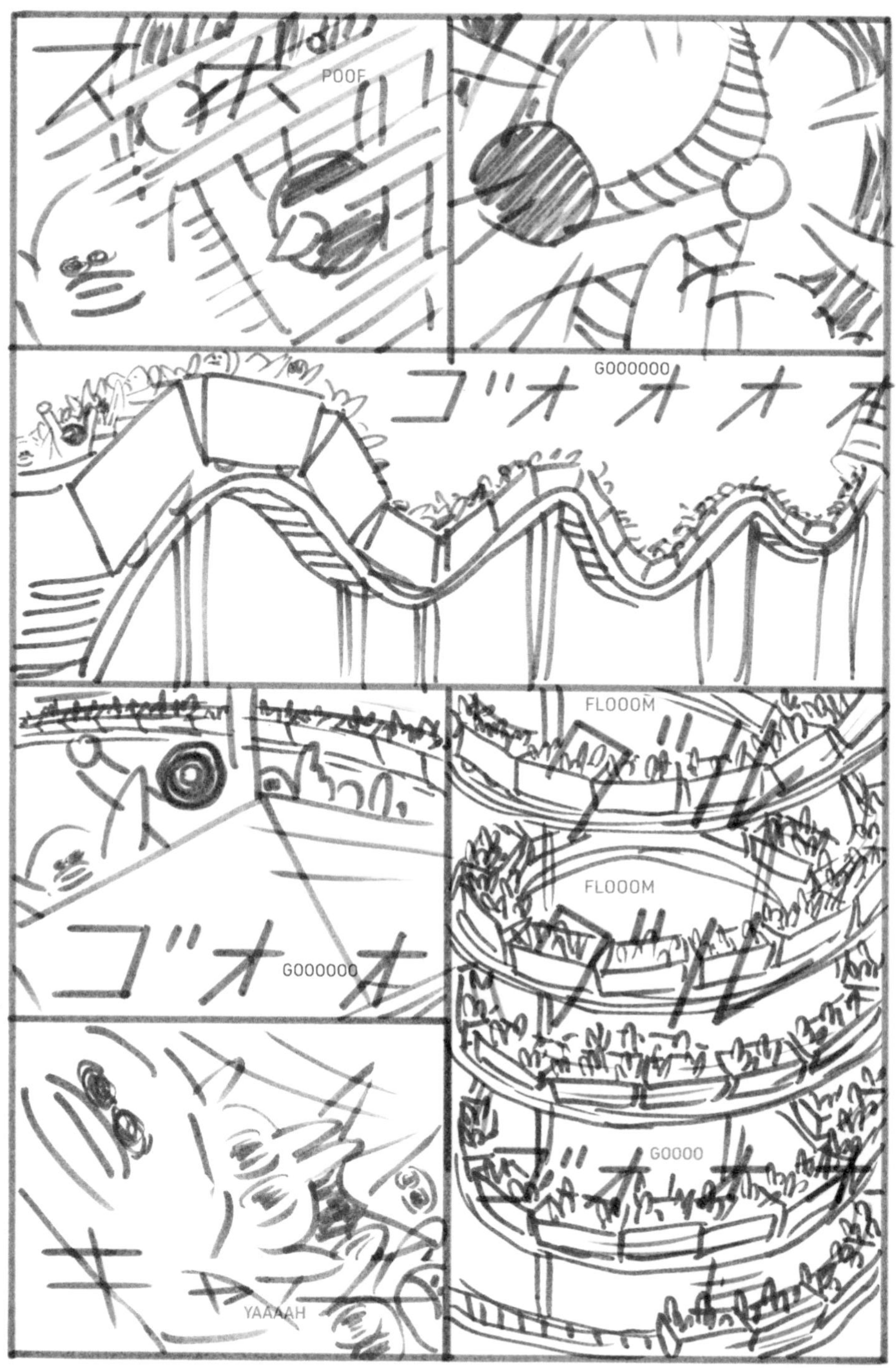
POOF
GOOOOOO
GOOOOOO
FLOOOM
FLOOOM
GOOOO
YAAAAH

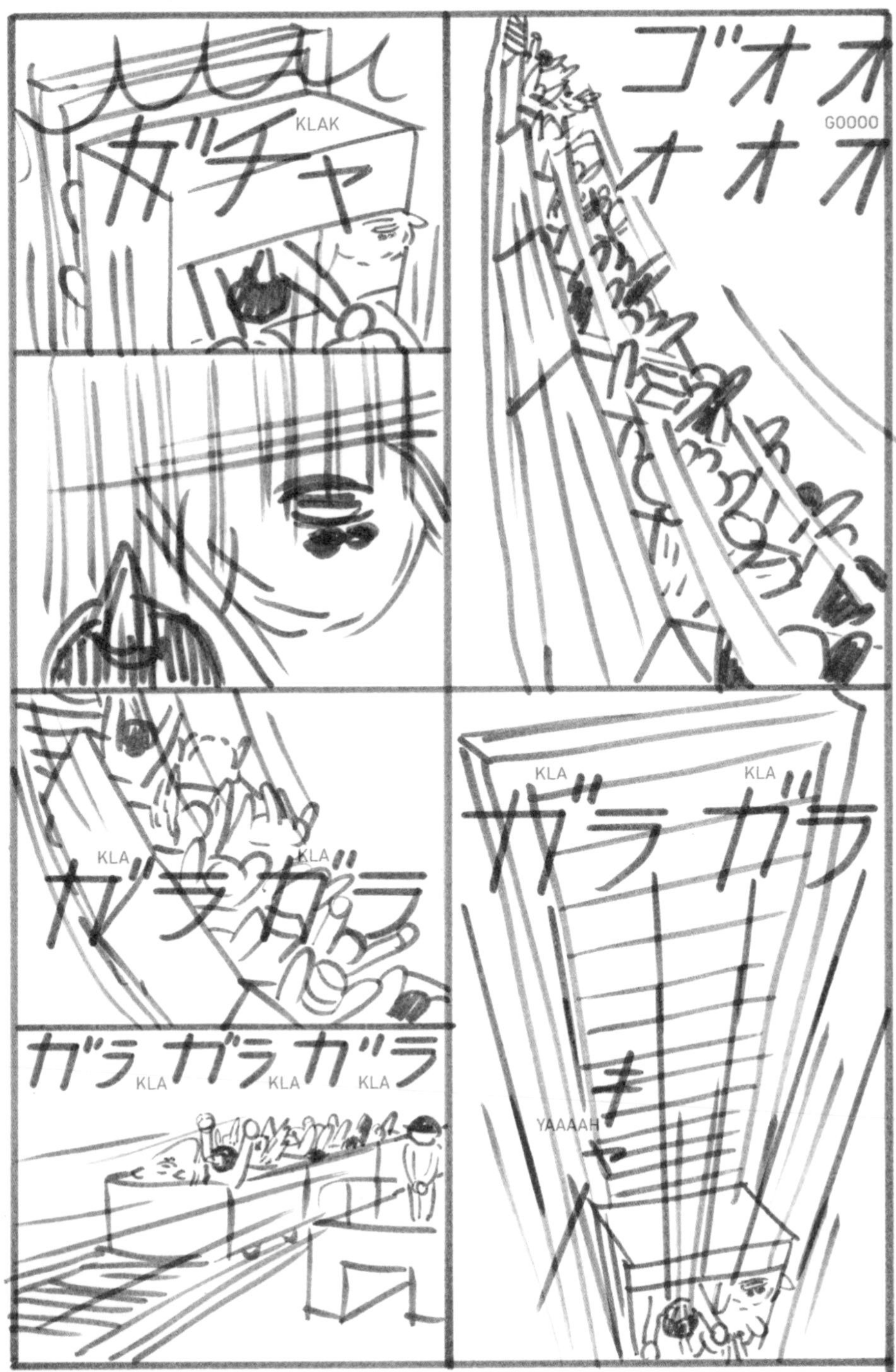

ゴオオオオオ
GOOOO
ガチャ
KLAK
ガラ ガラ
KLA
KLA
キャ
YAAAAH
ガラガラ
KLA
KLA
ガラ ガラ ガラ
KLA
KLA
KLA

WAAAA
WAAAA
ドス
POF
WAAAA
GWOOON
GWOOON

WAAAA
WAAAA
WAAAA
WAAAA
WAAAA
WAAAA
FLUM FLUM FLUM
WAAAA

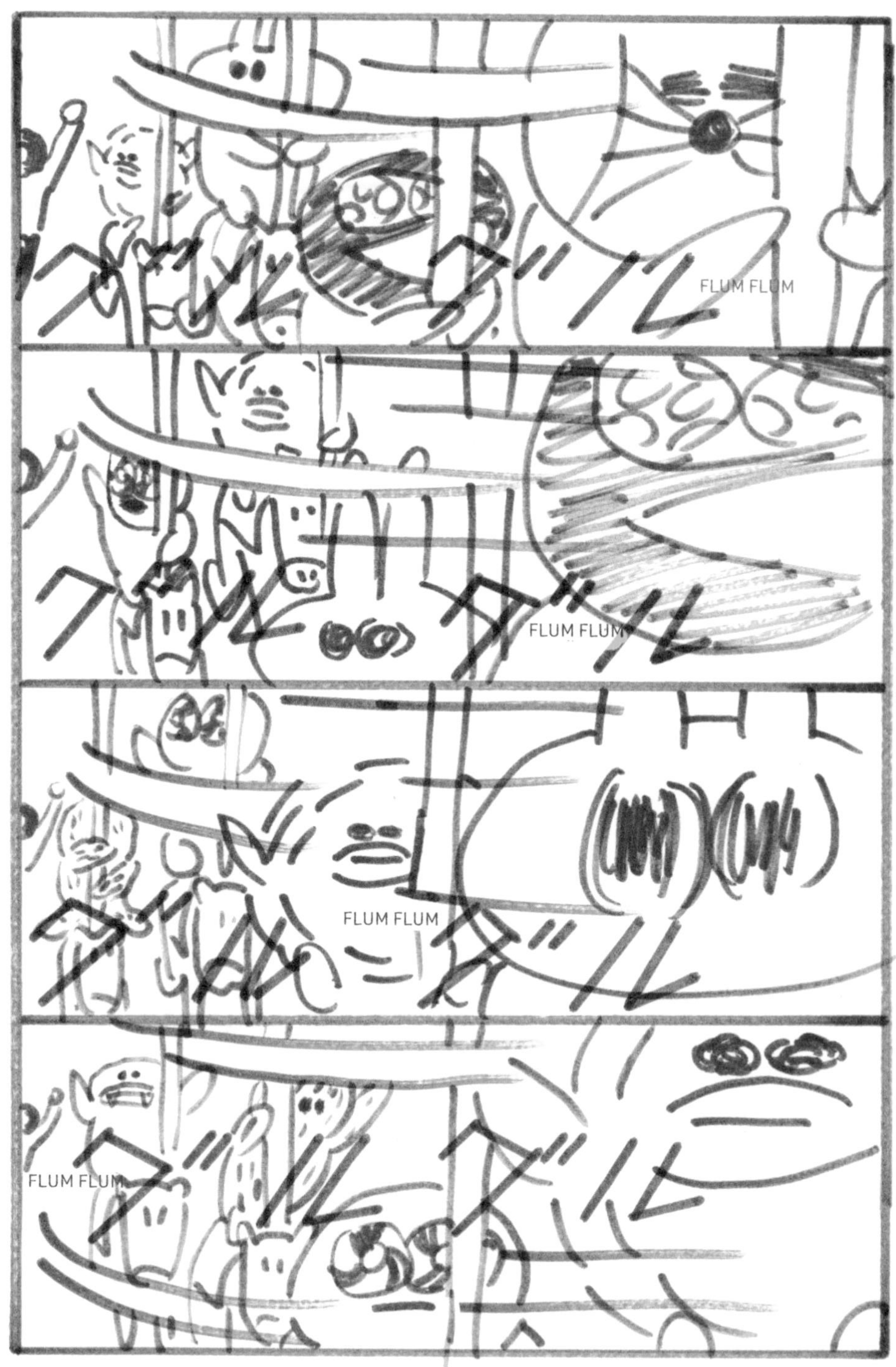
FLUM FLUM
FLUM FLUM
FLUM FLUM
FLUM FLUM

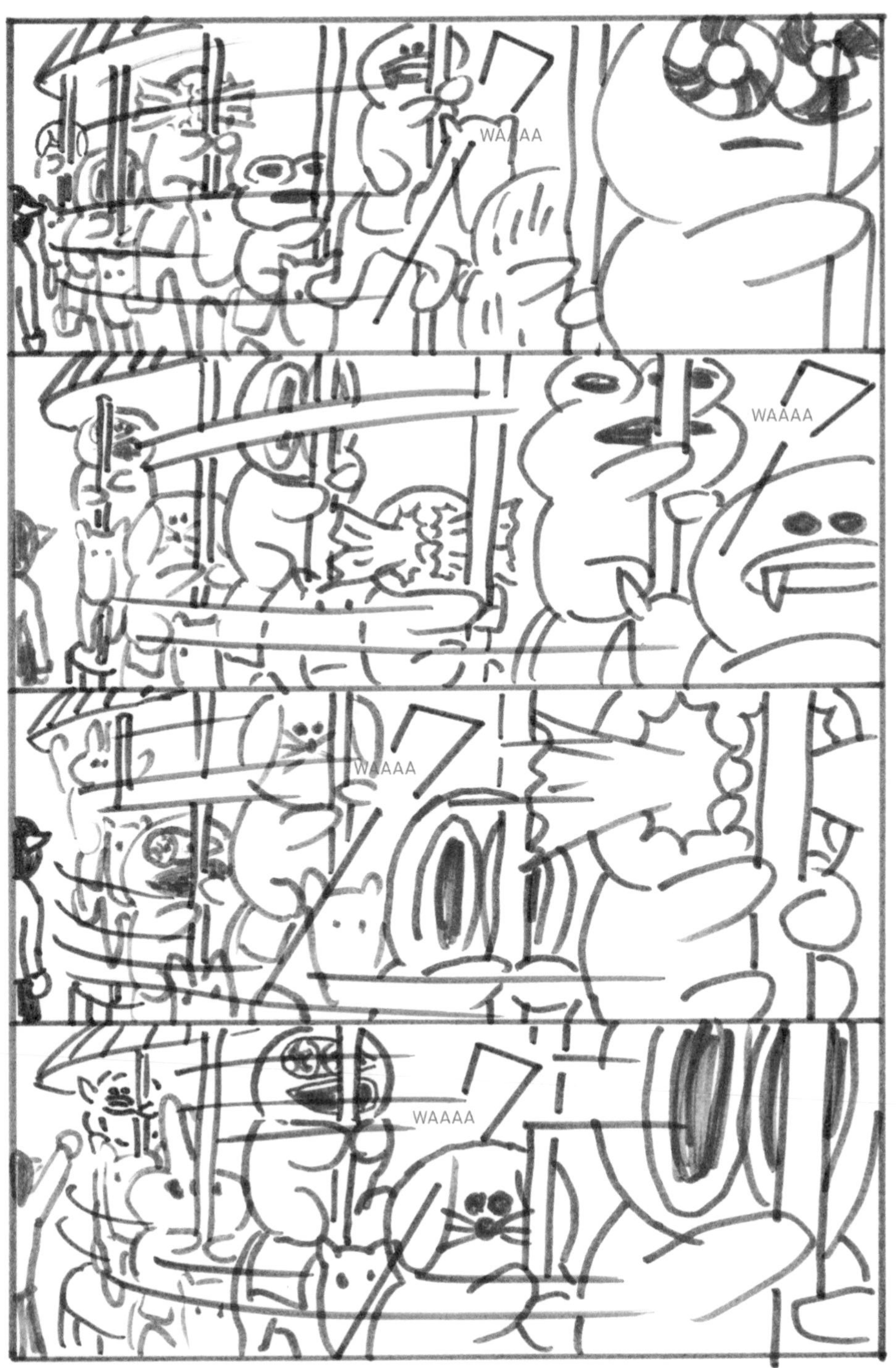
WAAAA
WAAAA
WAAAA
WAAAA

FSCHHH
BLOOSH
ZIP
TONG
FSCHHH
PAT
PAT
PAT
YAAH
YAAH

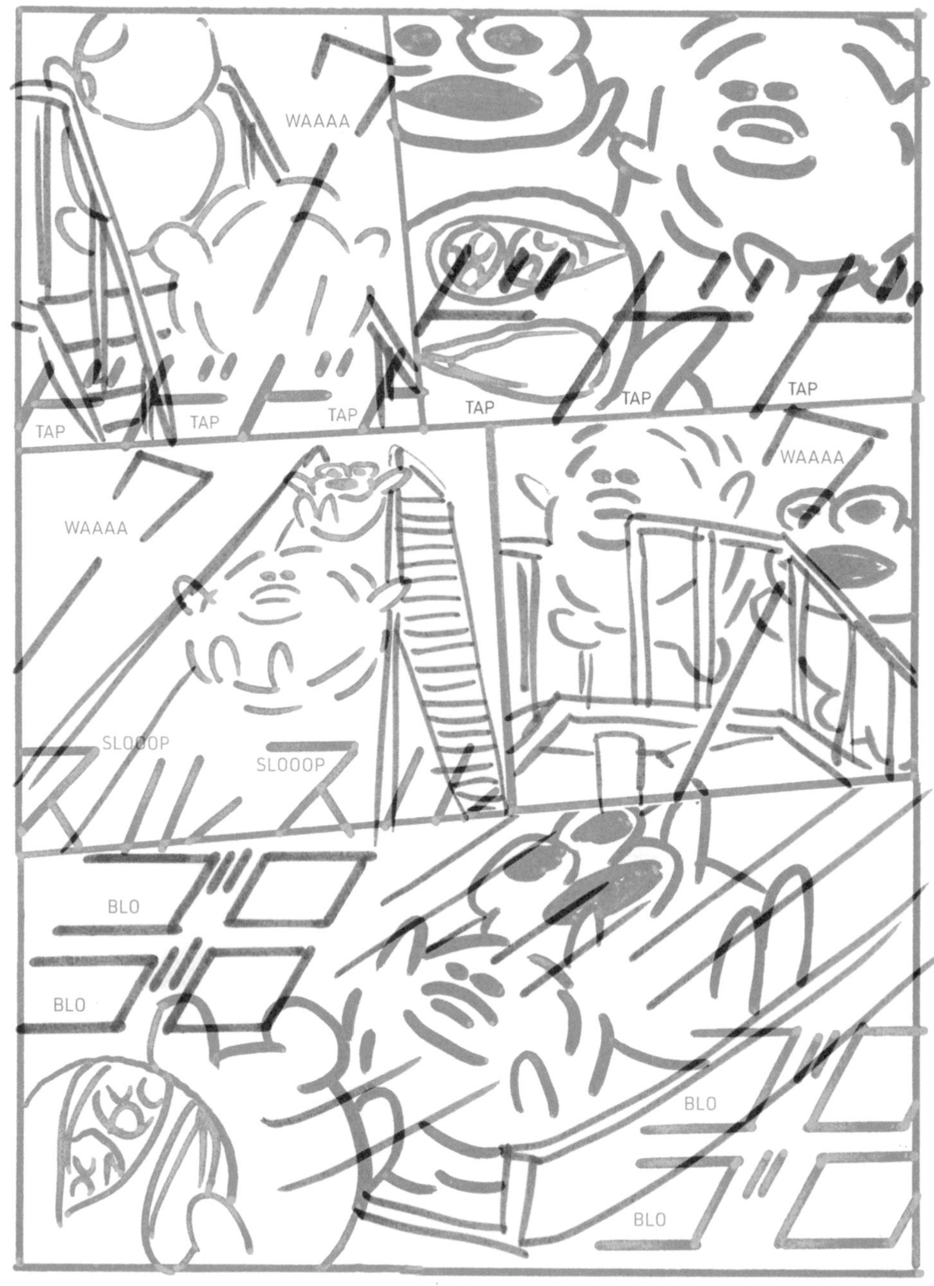
WAAAA
TAP
TAP
TAP
TAP
TAP
TAP
WAAAA
SLOOOP
SLOOOP
WAAAA
BLO
BLO
BLO
BLO

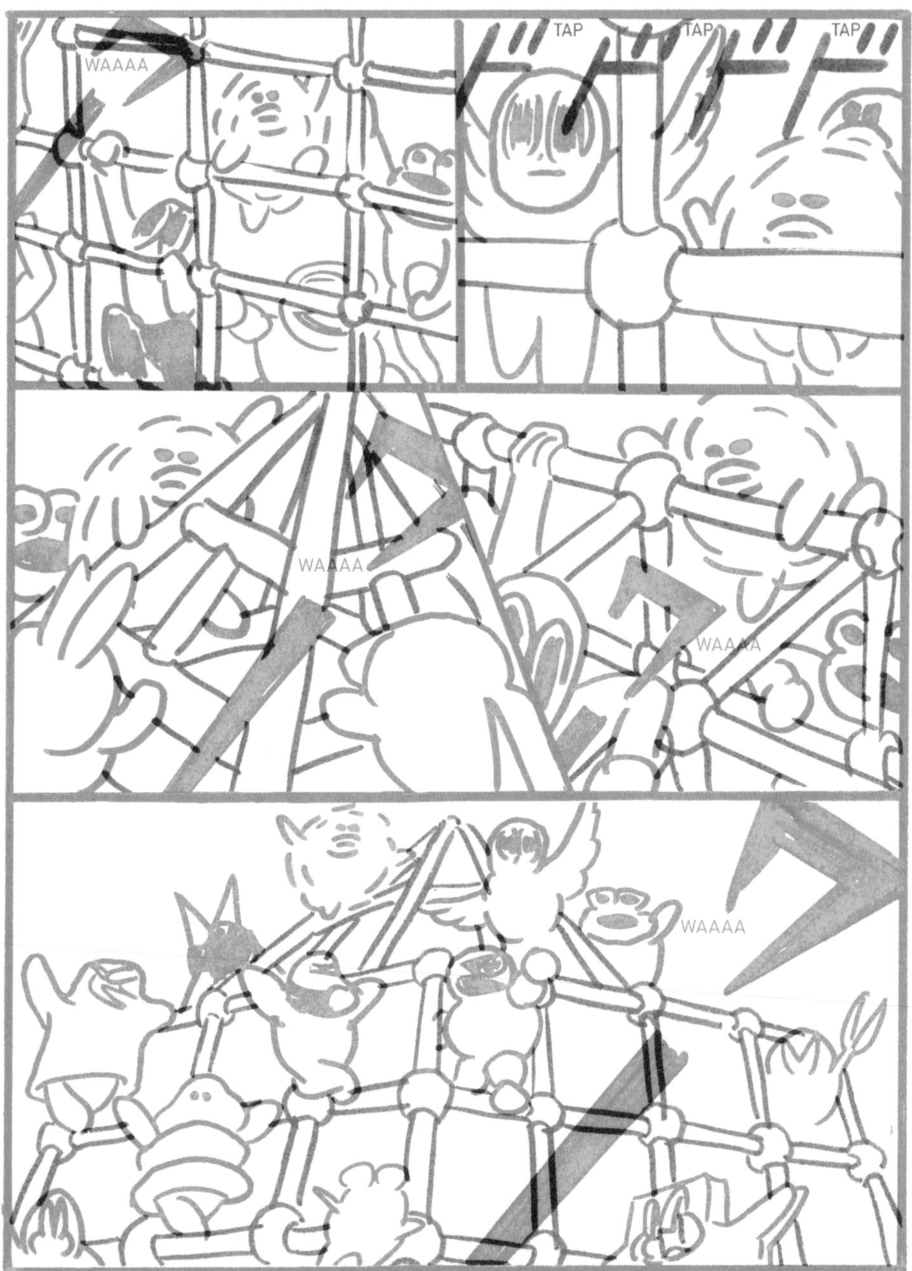
WAAAA
TAP
TAP
TAP
WAAAA
WAAAA
WAAAA

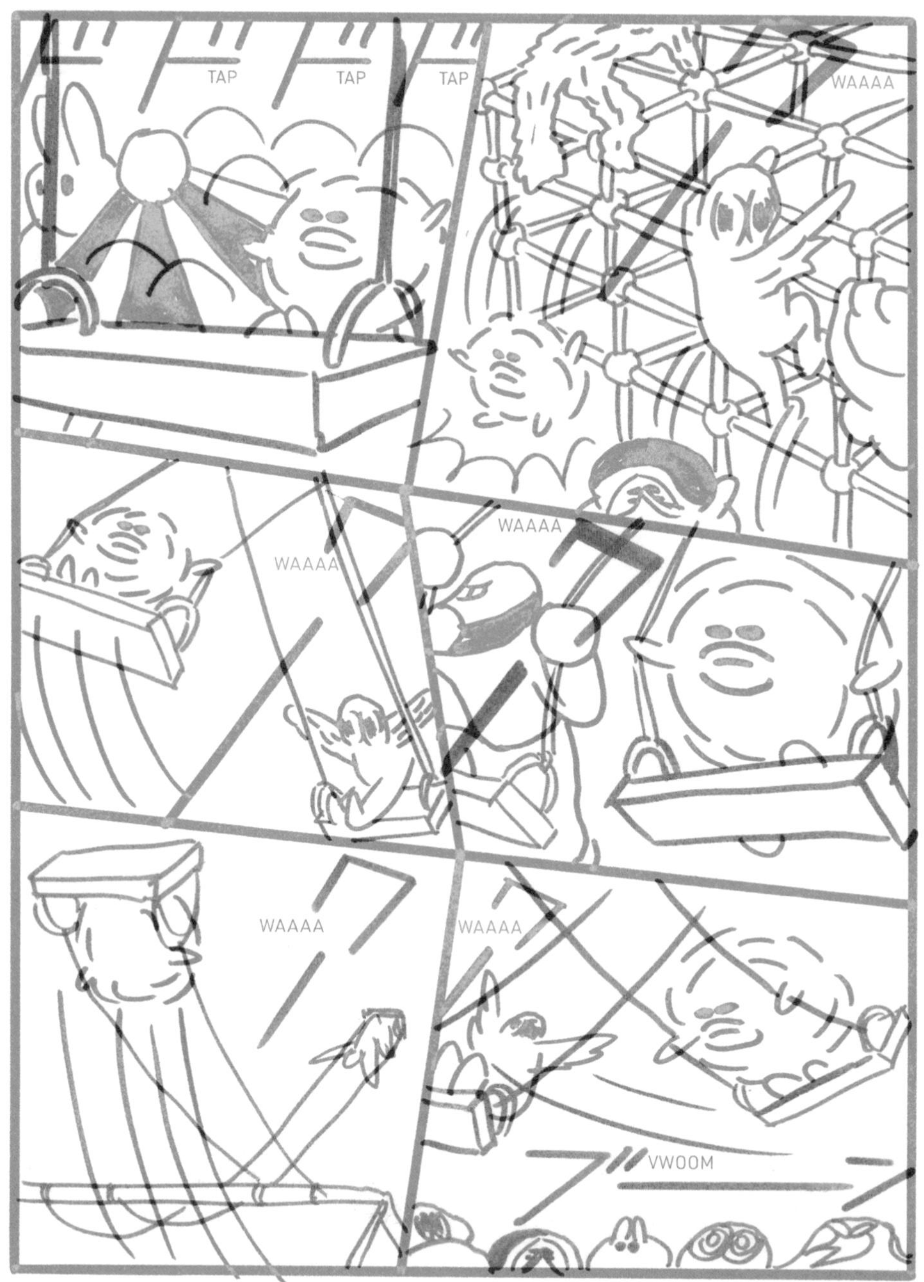
TAP
TAP
TAP
WAAAA
WAAAA
WAAAA
WAAAA
WAAAA
VWOOM

WAAAA
WAAAA
SHOOMP
FOOSH
WAAAA
SHOOMP
SHOOMP
SHOOMP
SHOOMP

SHUP
SHUP
SHUP
SHUP
SHUP
SHUP
ZHHK
SHUP
SHUP
SHUP
ペタ
PAT
ザラザラ
ZHK ZHK
ペタ
PAT

ZHK
ZHK
ZHK
ZHK
ZHK
ZHK
WAAAA
ZUB
WAAAA
ZUB

WAAAA
TAP
TAP
TAP
VROOOM
WAAAA
VROOOM
WAAAA
FWIP
FWIP
WAAAA
VROOOM
WAAAA

FWIP
FWIP
WAAAA
WAAAA
VROOOM
GONK
FWIP
FWIP
FWIP
FLUP
FLUP
FLUP

WAAAA
TAP
TAP
TAP
WAAAA
TAP
TAP
TAP
TAP
TAP
TAP
TAP
WAAAA
KIIIIIIII
BLO
BLO
BLO
BAM

TAP TAP TAP
WAAAA
WAAAA
WAAAA
TAP TAP TAP
SWIP

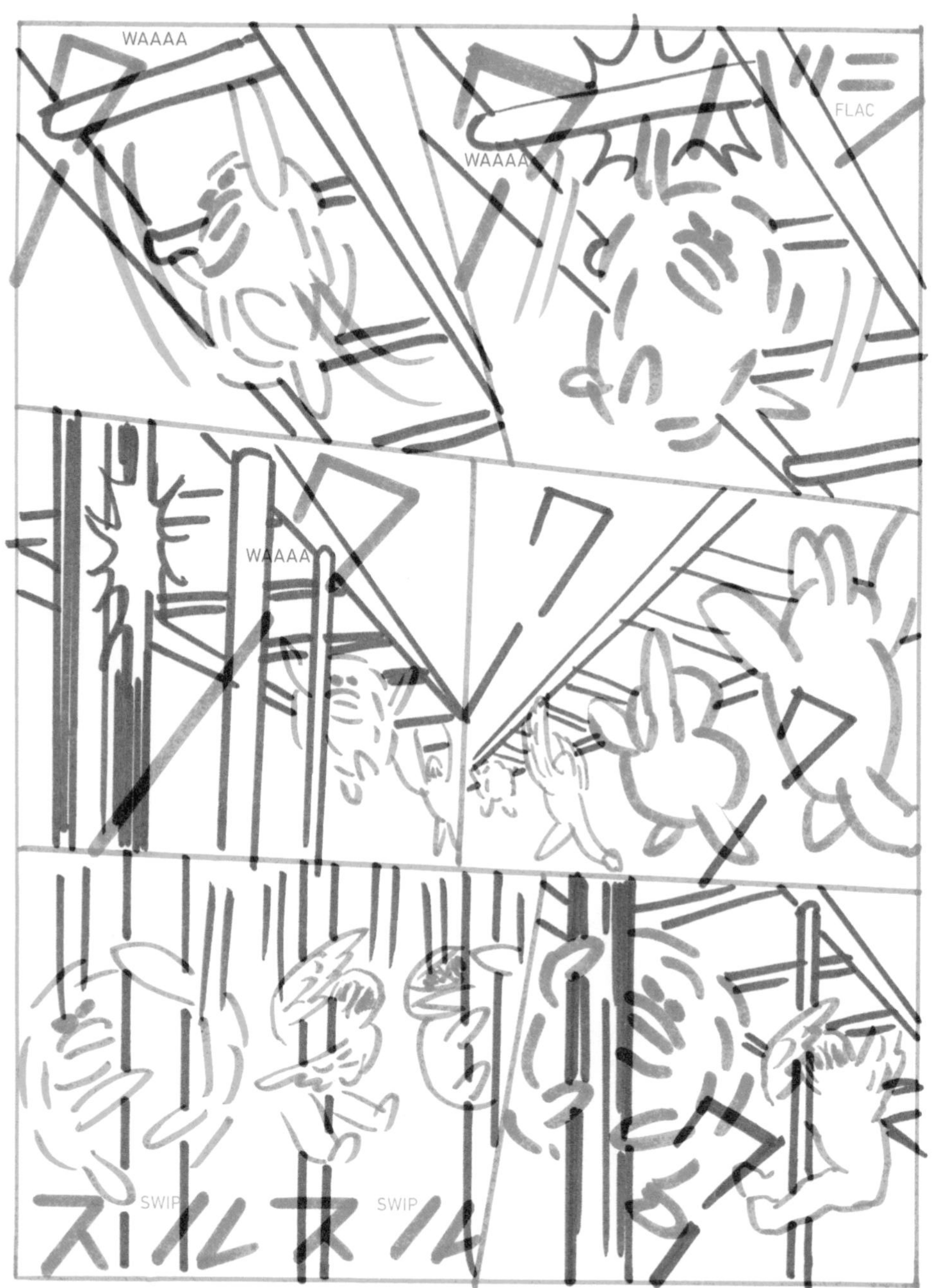
WAAAA
WAAAA
FLAC
WAAAA
SWIP
SWIP

POF
POF
SLU
SLU
FWIP
FWIP
FWIP
FWIP
POF
POF
POF
POF

WAAAA
TAP
TAP
TAP
WAAAA
TAP
TAP
TAP
WAAAA
TAP
TAP
WAAAA
WAAAA
TAP
TAP
TAP
TAP
TAP

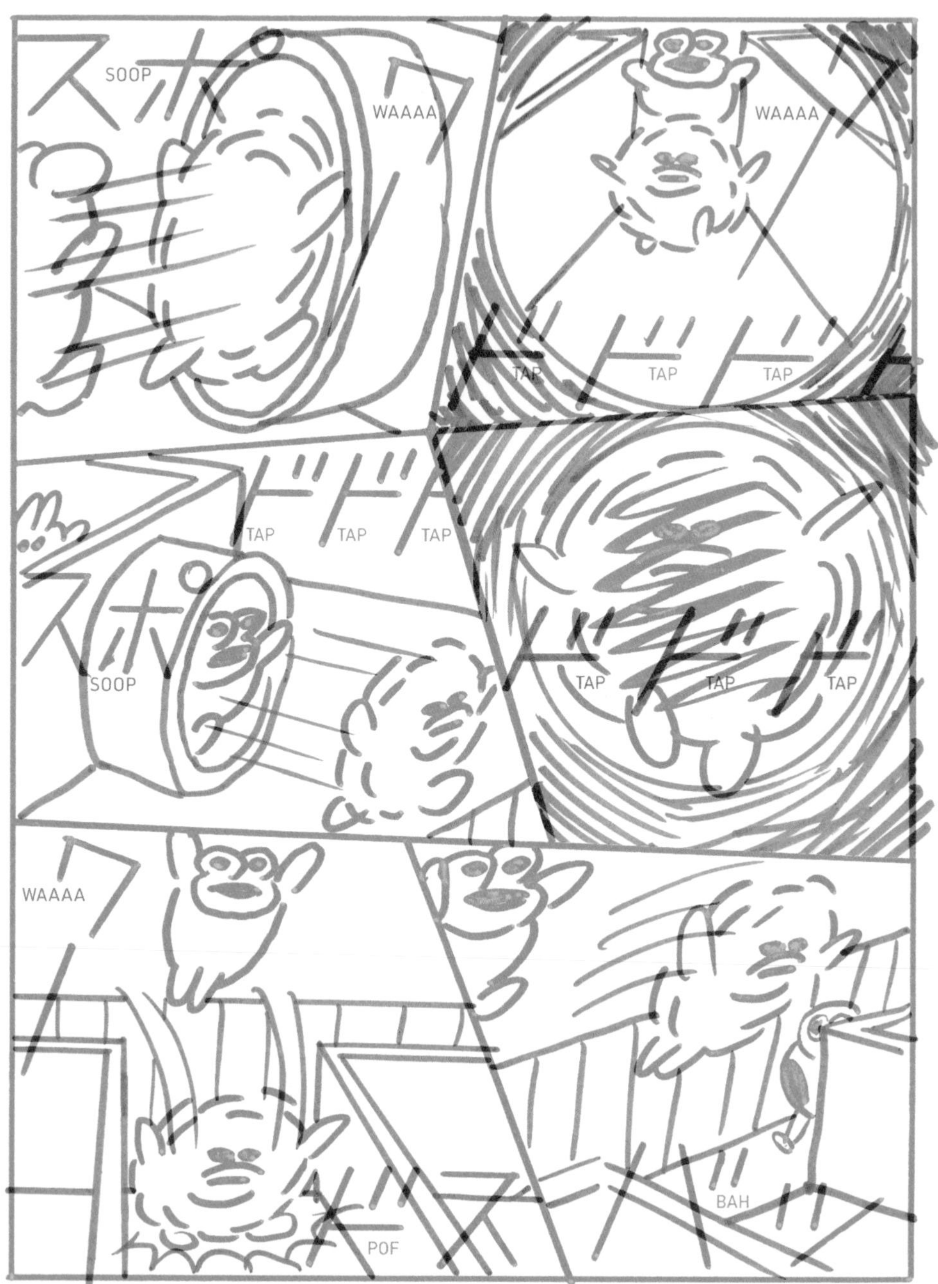

SOOP
WAAAA
WAAAA
TAP TAP TAP
TAP TAP TAP
SOOP
TAP TAP TAP
WAAAA
POF
BAH

TAP
TAP
TAP
WAAAA
WAAAA
TAP
TAP
TAP
SOOP
WAAAA
TAP
TAP
TAP
WAAAA
SOOP
ZIP

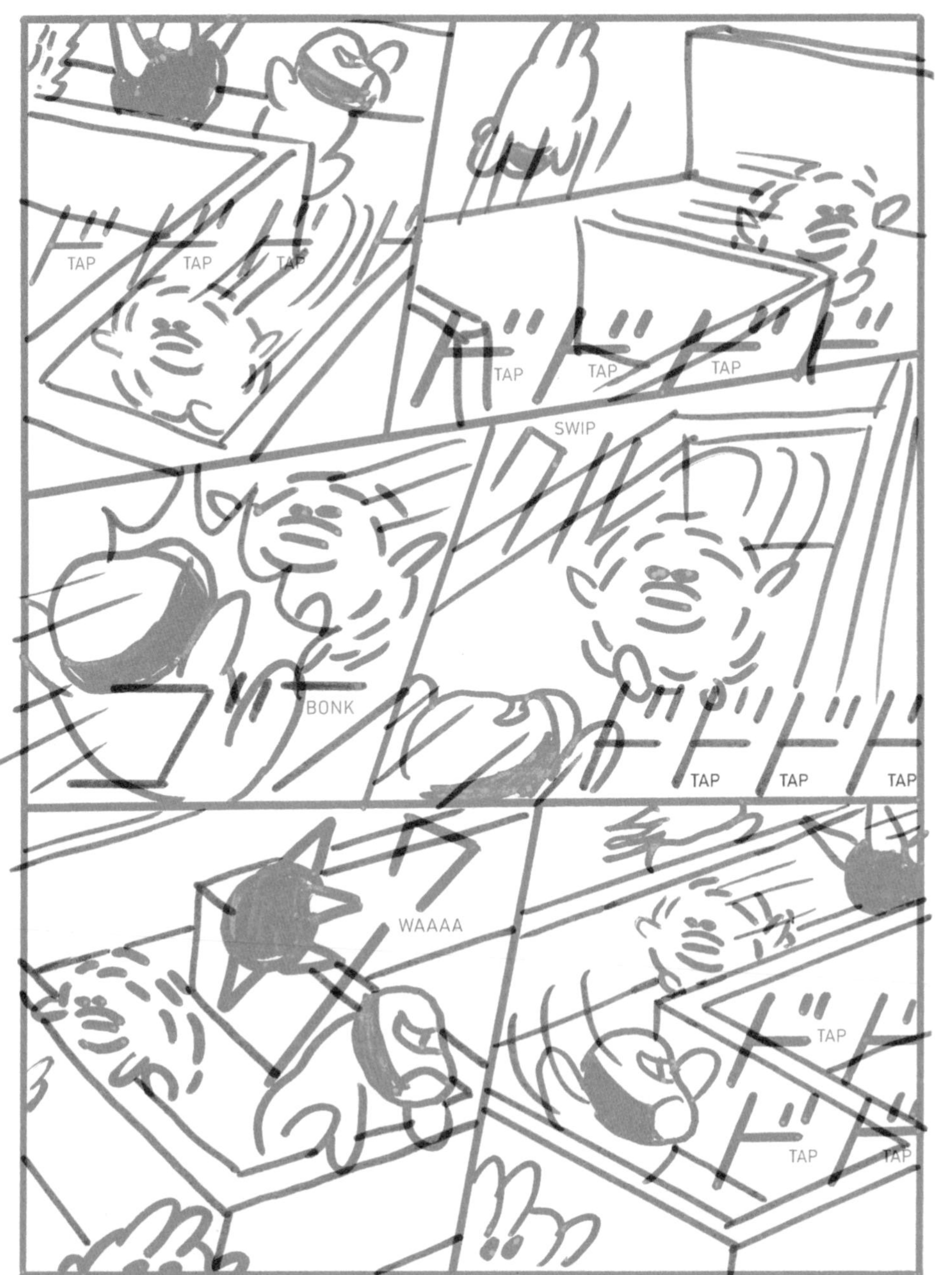
TAP TAP TAP
TAP TAP TAP
SWIP
BONK
TAP TAP TAP
WAAAA
TAP
TAP TAP

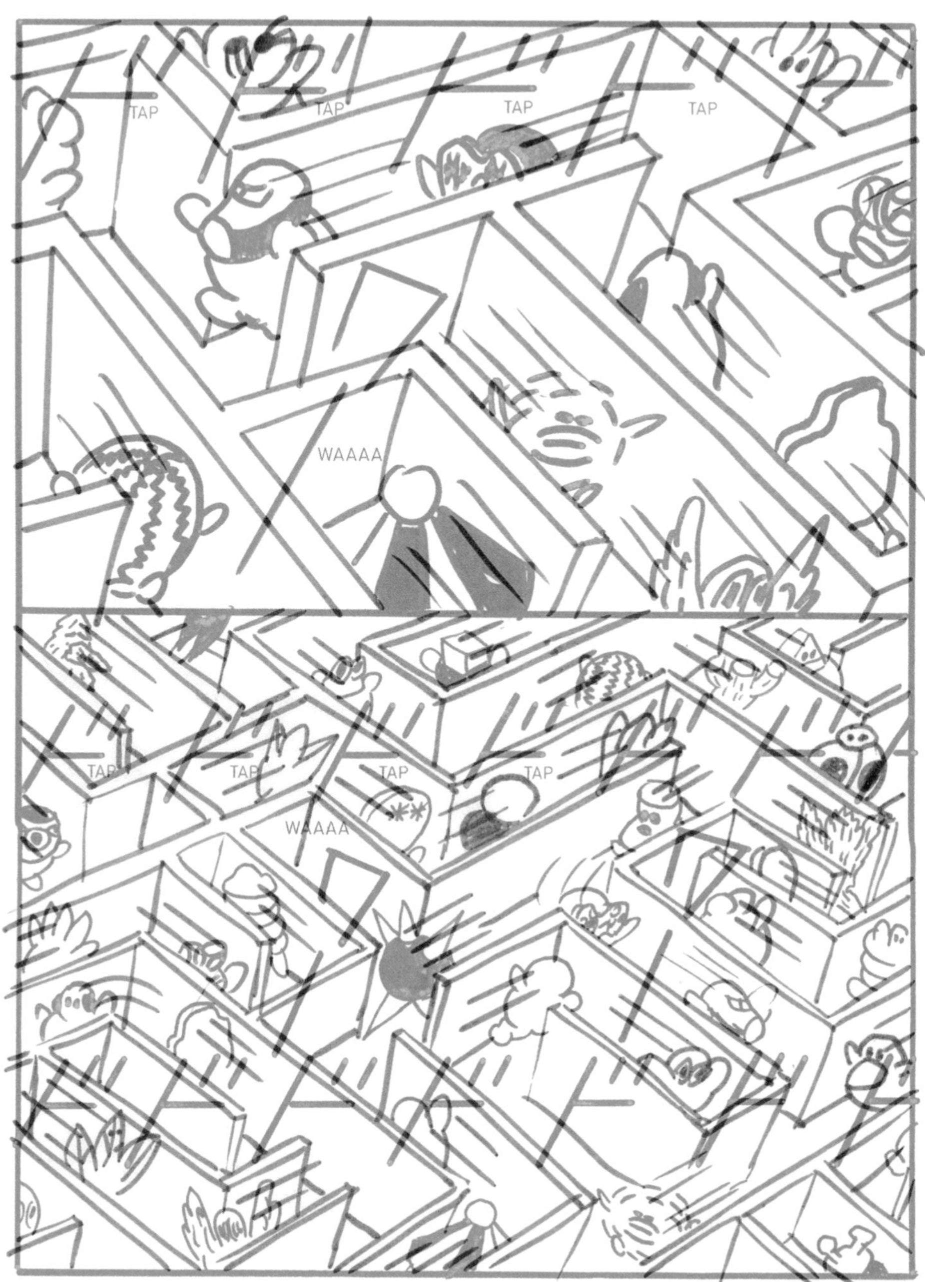
TAP
TAP
TAP
TAP
WAAAA
TAP
TAP
TAP
TAP
WAAAA

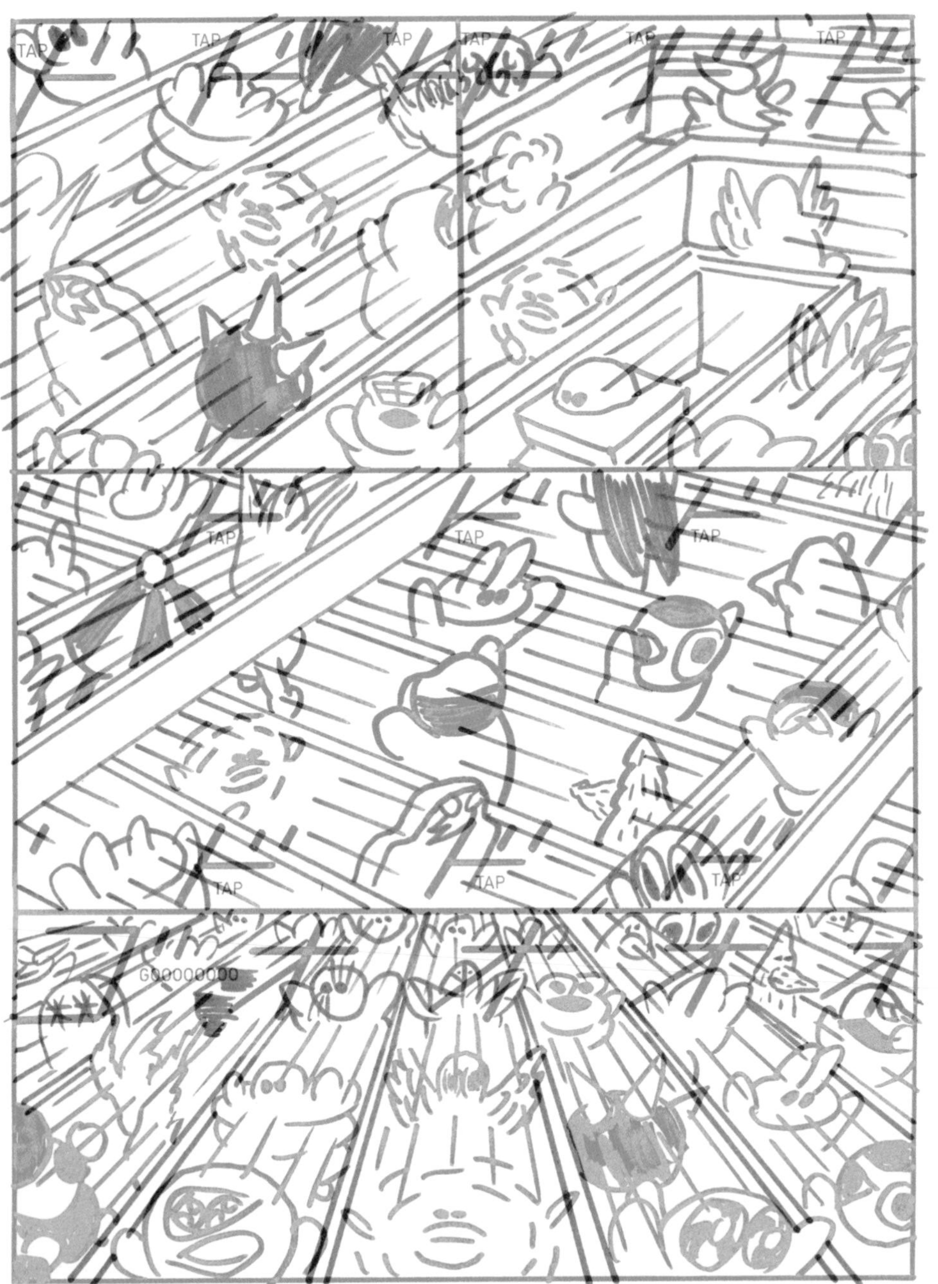
TAP
TAP
TAP
TAP
TAP
TAP
TAP
TAP
TAP
TAP
TAP
TAP
GOOOOOOOO

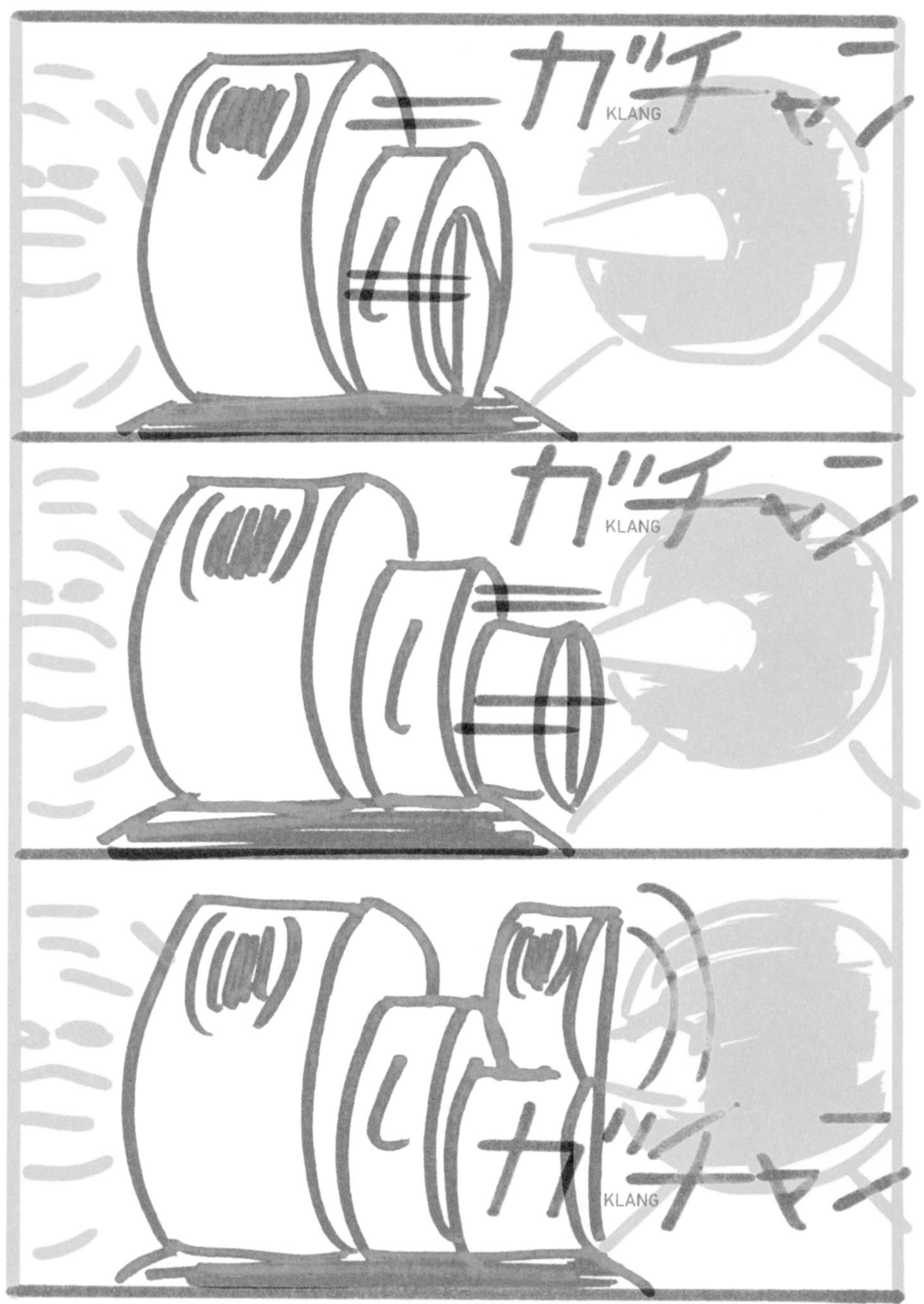
KLANG
KLANG
KLANG

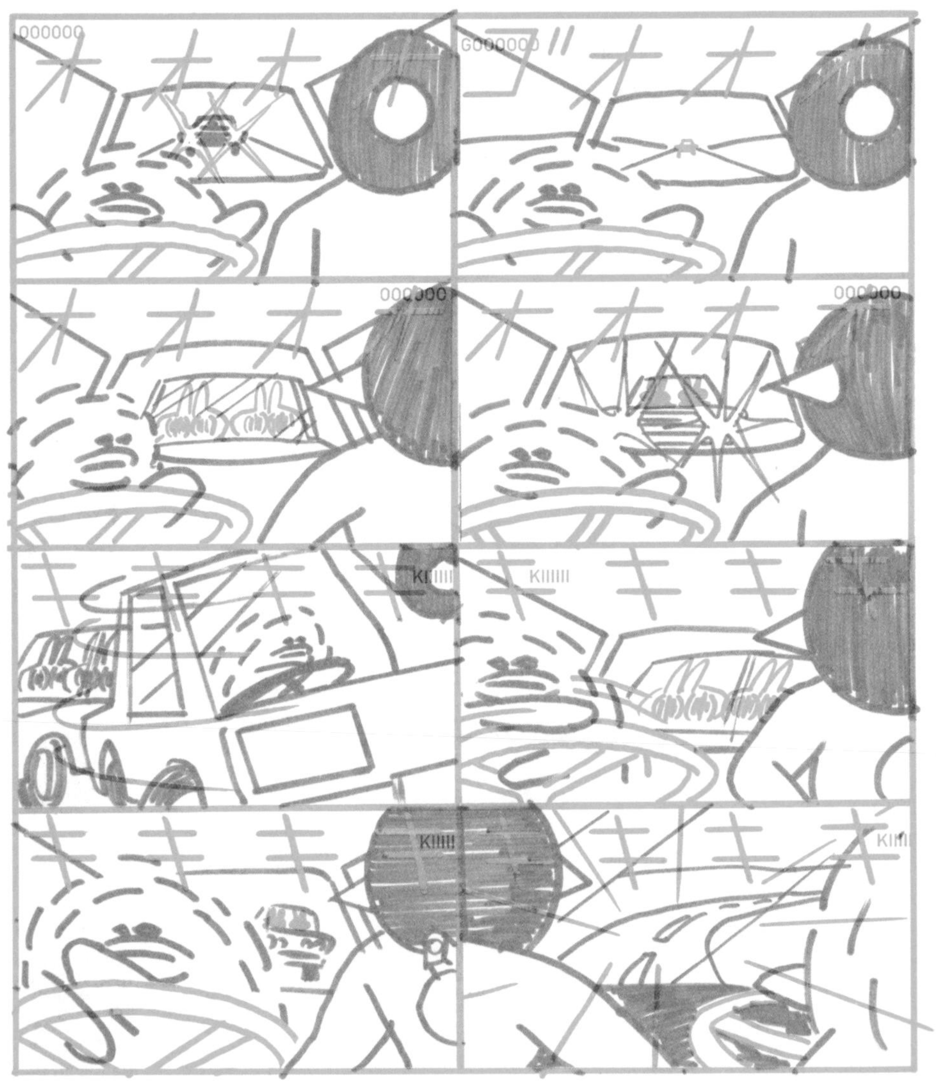
GOOOOOO
OOOOOO
OOOOOO
OOOOOO
KIIIII
KIIIII
KIIII
KIIII!

ゴソゴソ
CLING CLING
パク
SPUK
ザブ
BLOOP
パカ
PLAC
パーッ
PWAAAA
パーッ
PWAAAA
ドドド
TAP TAP TAP

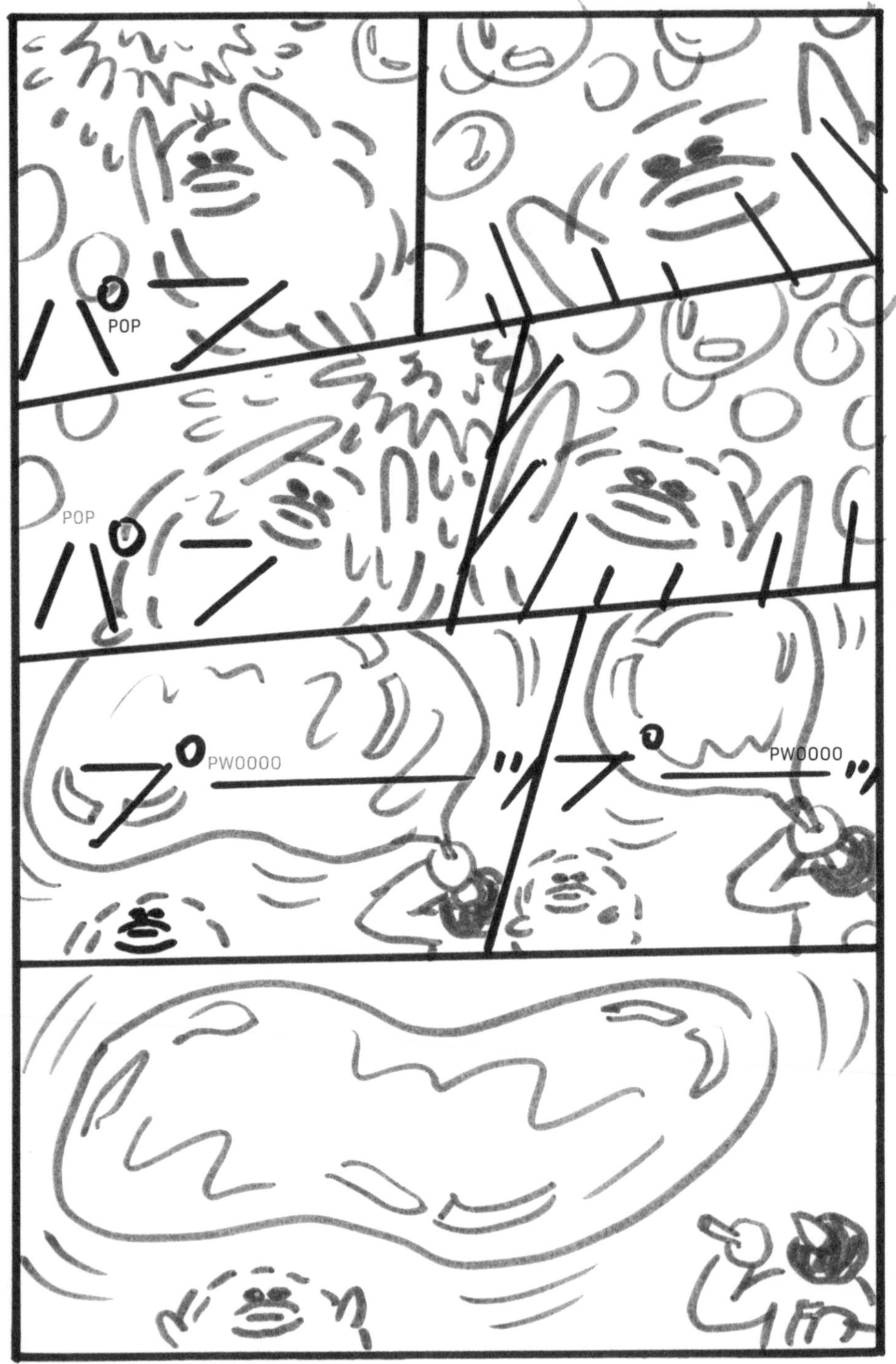
パーン
POP
パーン
POP
PWOOOO
PWOOOO

ズボ
ZBLOOP
パク
SPUK
プーーッ
PFOOOO
ズボ
ZBLOOP
プーーッ
PFOOOO
ズボ
ZBLOOP
プー
PFOOOO
プー
PFOOOO

ガラガラ
KLA KLA
ドドド
TAP TAP TAP

ビュッ
VWOOM
ブーン
VWWW
ガバッ
HRRP
BAM
バン
SCHLL
SCHLL
FWUP
FWUP
ビュッ
VWOOM
ガバッ
ビシュ
VWOOSH
ガバッ
HRRP
バシ
BAP
HRRP
ガバ
バシ
BAP
SCHLL
SCHLL

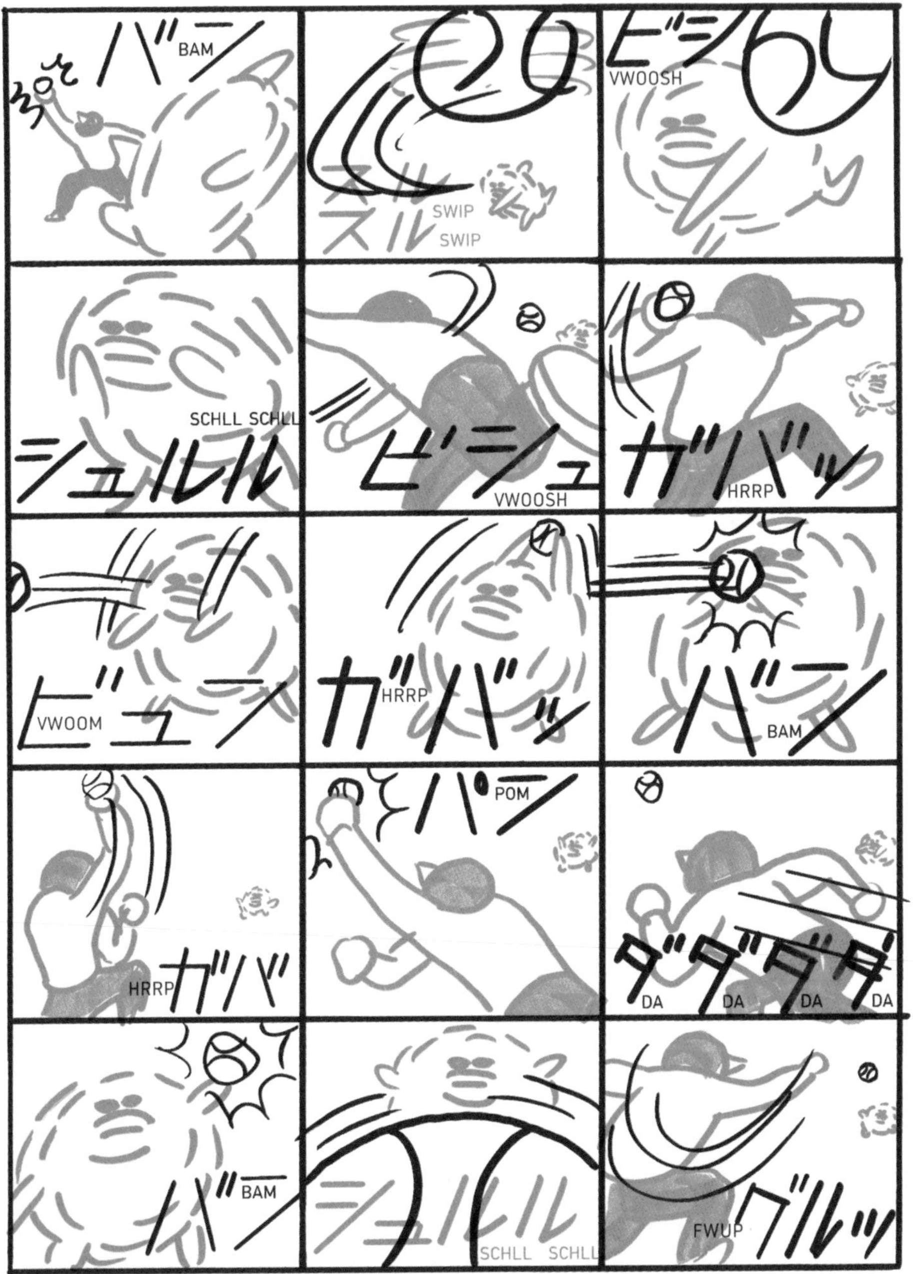

バーン
BAM
スルスル
SWIP
SWIP
VWOOSH
シュルルル
SCHLL SCHLL
ビシュ
VWOOSH
ガバッ
HRRP
ビューン
VWOOM
ガバッ
HRRP
バーン
BAM
HRRP
ガバ
パーン
POM
ダダダダ
DA DA DA DA
バーン
BAM
シュルルル
SCHLL SCHLL
FWUP
グルッ

GWEEEN
VWOOSH
HRRP
BAM
BAM
POM
PWIP
BAM
TAP
TAP
TAP
POM
TAP
TAP
TAP
FWUP
FWUP
PAPAM
SPAP
HRRP

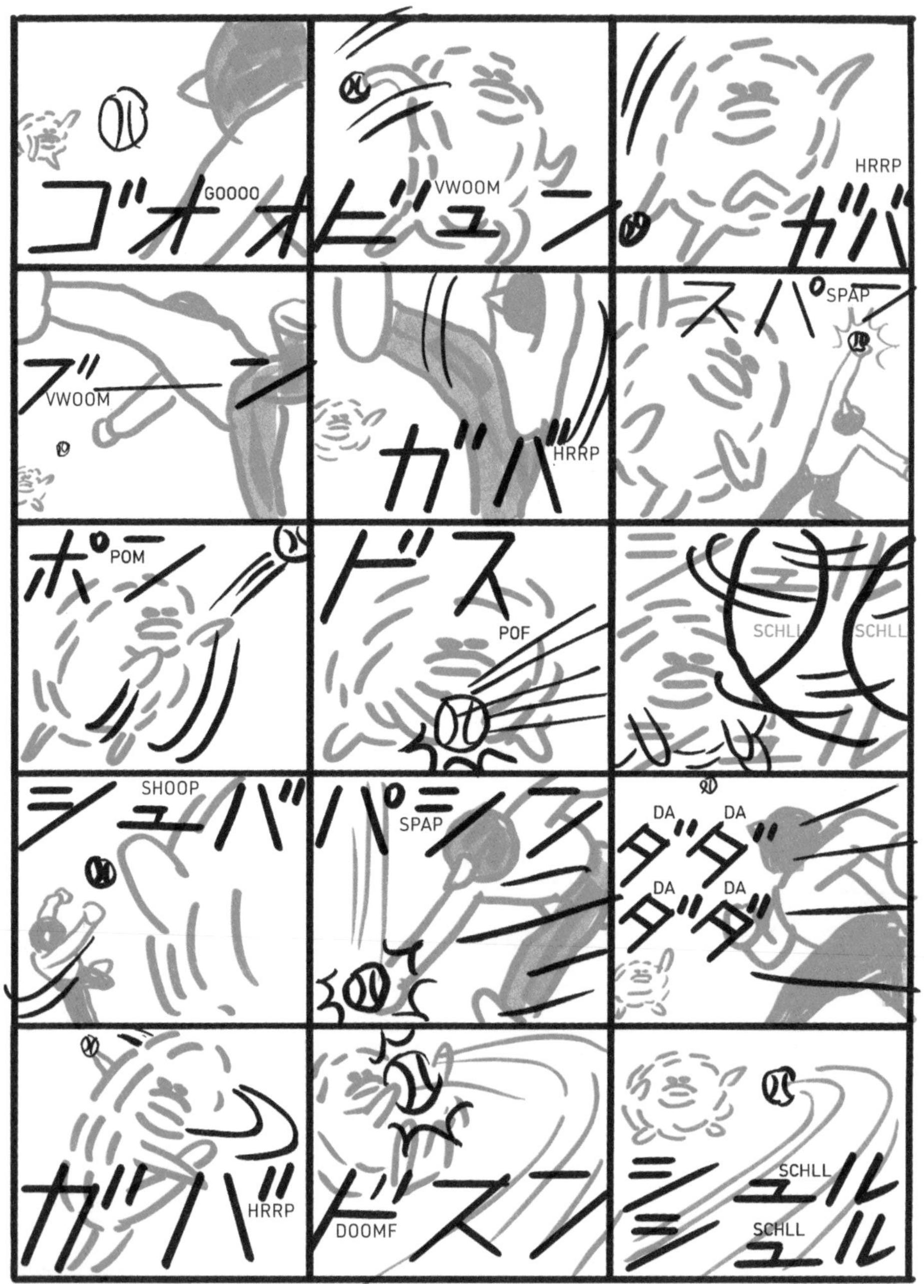

ゴオオ
GOOOO
ビューン
VWOOM
ガバ
HRRP
ブーン
VWOOM
ガバ
HRRP
スパ
SPAP
ポーン
POM
ドス
POF
SCHLL
SCHLL
シュバ
SHOOP
SPAP
DA
DA
DA
DA
HRRP
DOOMF
SCHLL
SCHLL

POM
TAP TAP TAP
VWOOSH
BLOM BLOM
BONG
シュルル
SCHLL
SHOOP
VWOOM
BAM
ゴロゴロゴロ
BLOM BLOM BLOM
VWOOM
BAF
PLOM PLOM PLOM
BAF
ダダダ
DA DA DA
BLOM BLOM
ゴロゴロ
PLOM PLOM PLOM

シュルル
SCHLL
TAP TAP TAP
SCHLL
シュルル
POOOM
TAP TAP TAP
POOOM
FSSSSS
POOOM
POOOM
POOOM
BTUM
BAM
VWOOM
PAM
VWOOM
BAF
ゴロゴロ
BLOM BLOM
ゴロゴロ

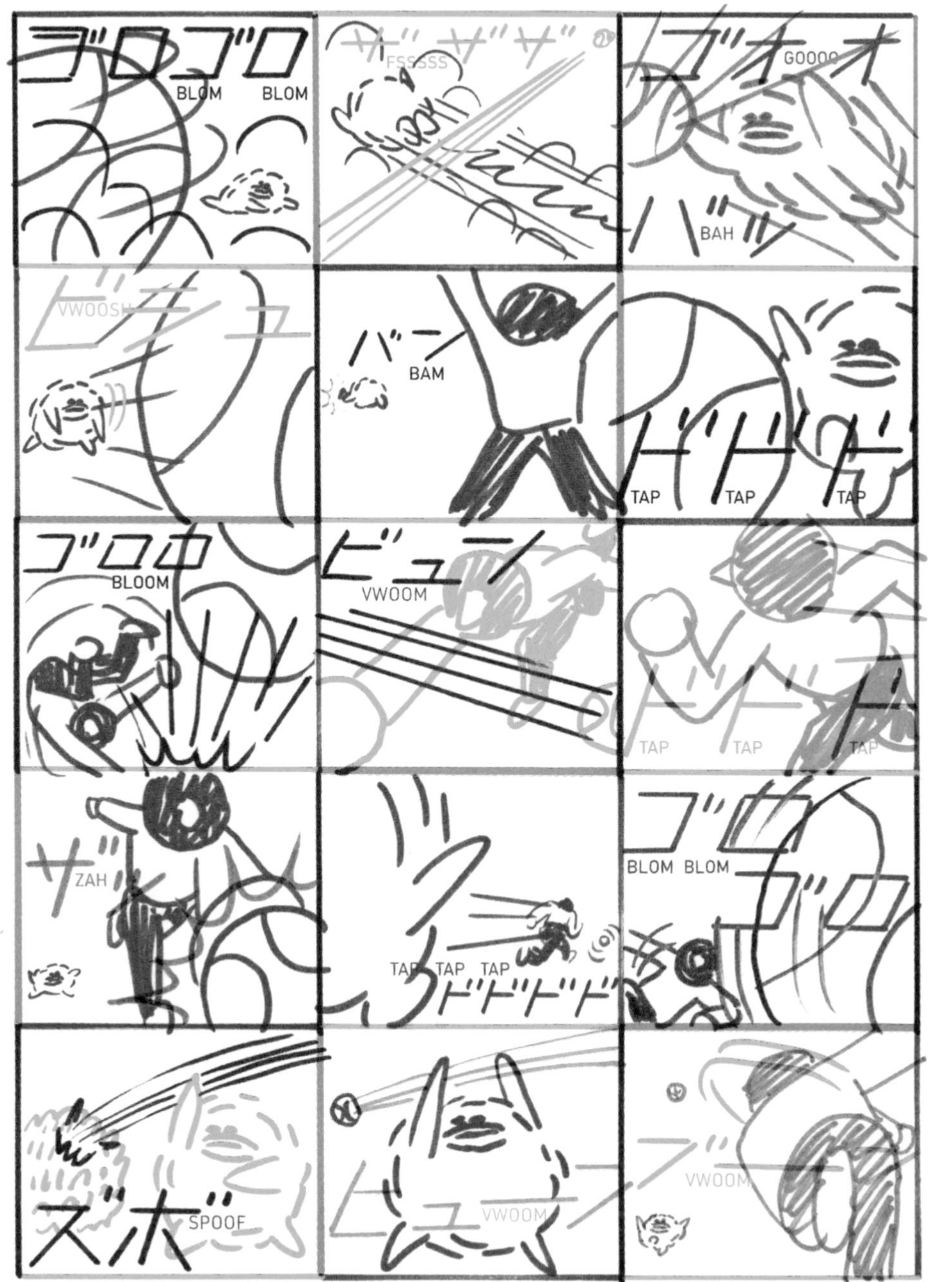

ゴロゴロ
BLOM BLOM
ザザザ
FSSSSS
ゴオオ
GOOOO
バッ
BAH
ビューン
VWOOSH
バッ
BAM
ドドド
TAP TAP TAP
ゴロロ
BLOOM
ビューン
VWOOM
ドドド
TAP TAP TAP
ザ
ZAH
TAP TAP TAP
ドドドドド
ゴロゴロ
BLOM BLOM
ズボ
SPOOF
ビュー
VWOOM
VWOOM

ガサガサ
FRISH FRISH
ガサガサ
ガサ ガサ
FRISH FRISH
ドドドド
TAP TAP TAP
ガサガサ
ガサガサ
FRISH FRISH
ポーン
POOM
ガバッ
HRRP
ドドドド
TAP TAP TAP
バッ
BAH
ドブーン
SPLOOSH

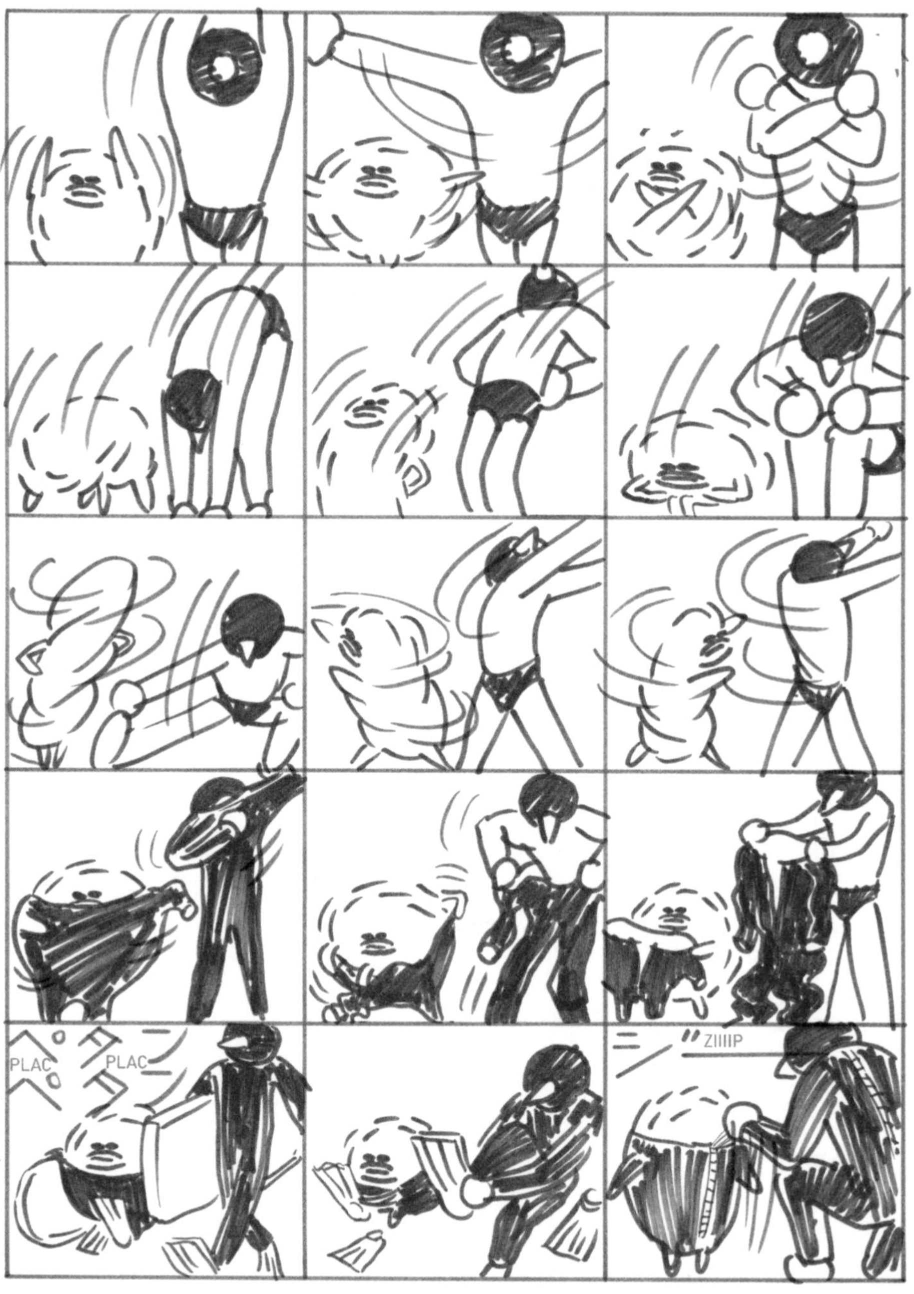
PLAC
PLAC
ZIIIIP

FSCH
FSCH
SPLASH
SPLASH
BA
BA
BA
BA
BA
BA
BA
BA
BA
FLUP
FLUP
FSCH
FSCH
FSCH
FSCH
ZBLOOSH
GOOO
BA
BA
BA
FSCHLL
GOOO
BLUB
BLUB

BA
BA
BA
BA
DA
DA
DA
DA
DA
DA
DA
DA

FRISH
FRISH
DA
DA
DA
VOUUUM
SLL
SLL

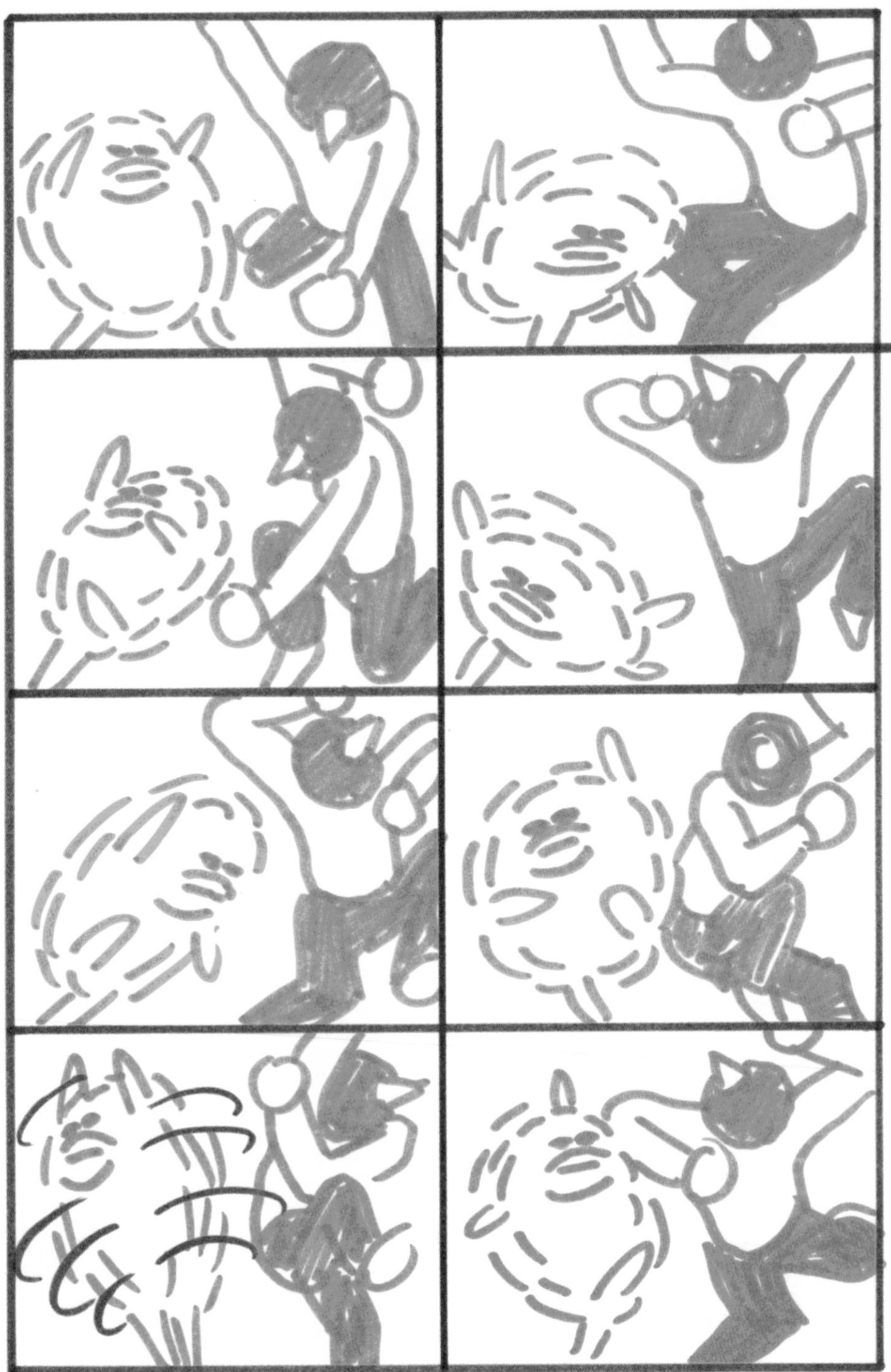

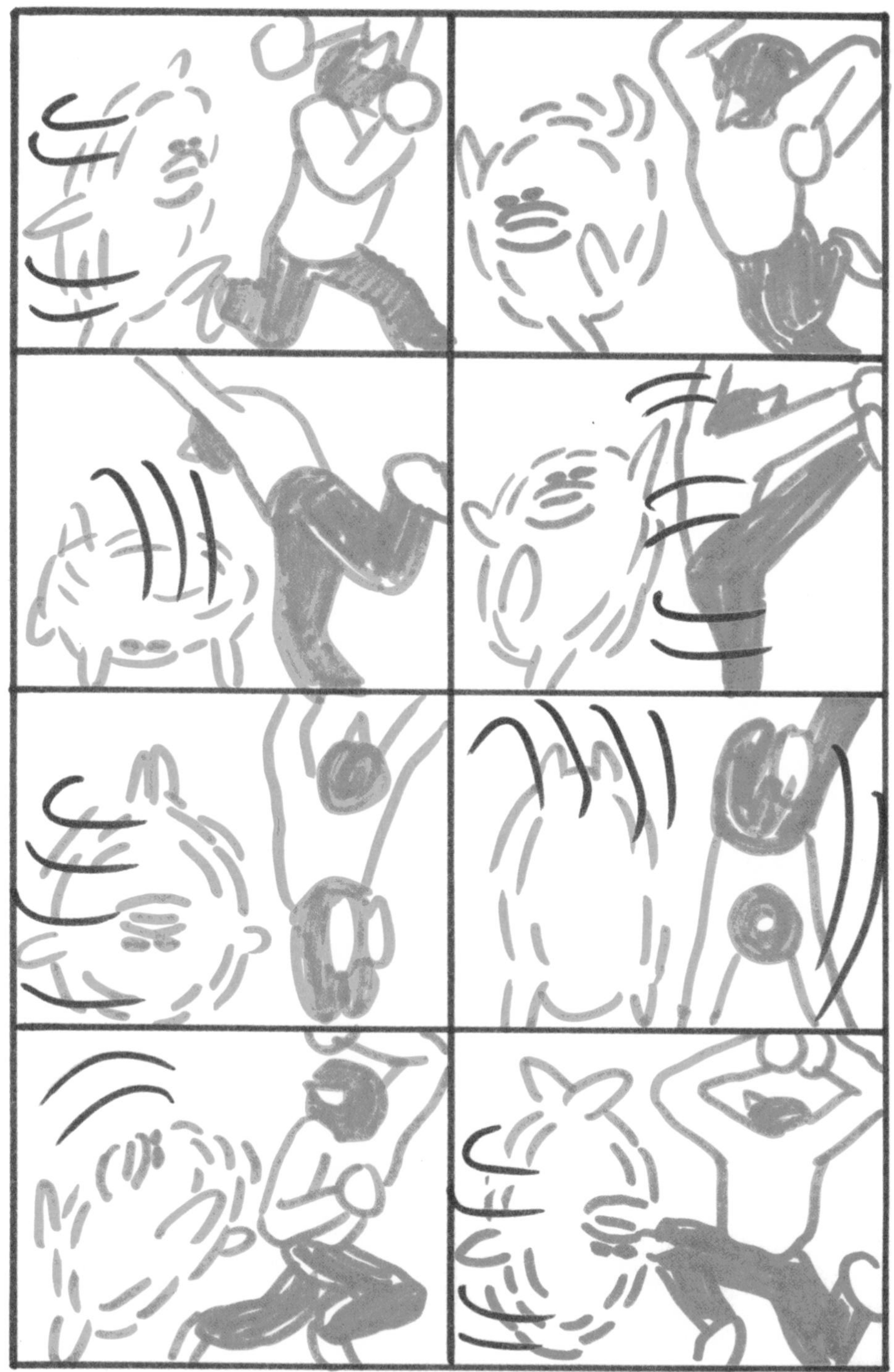

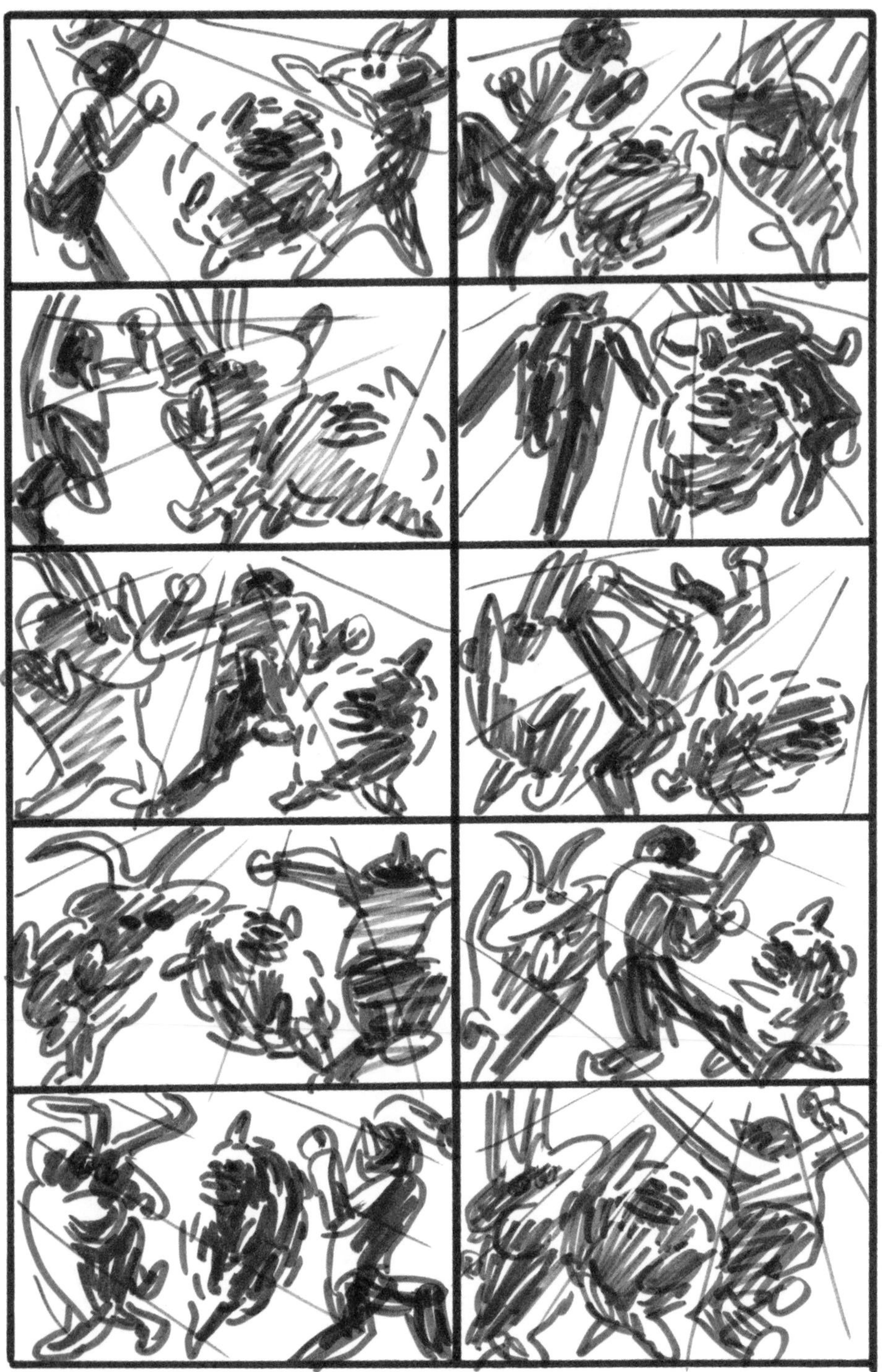

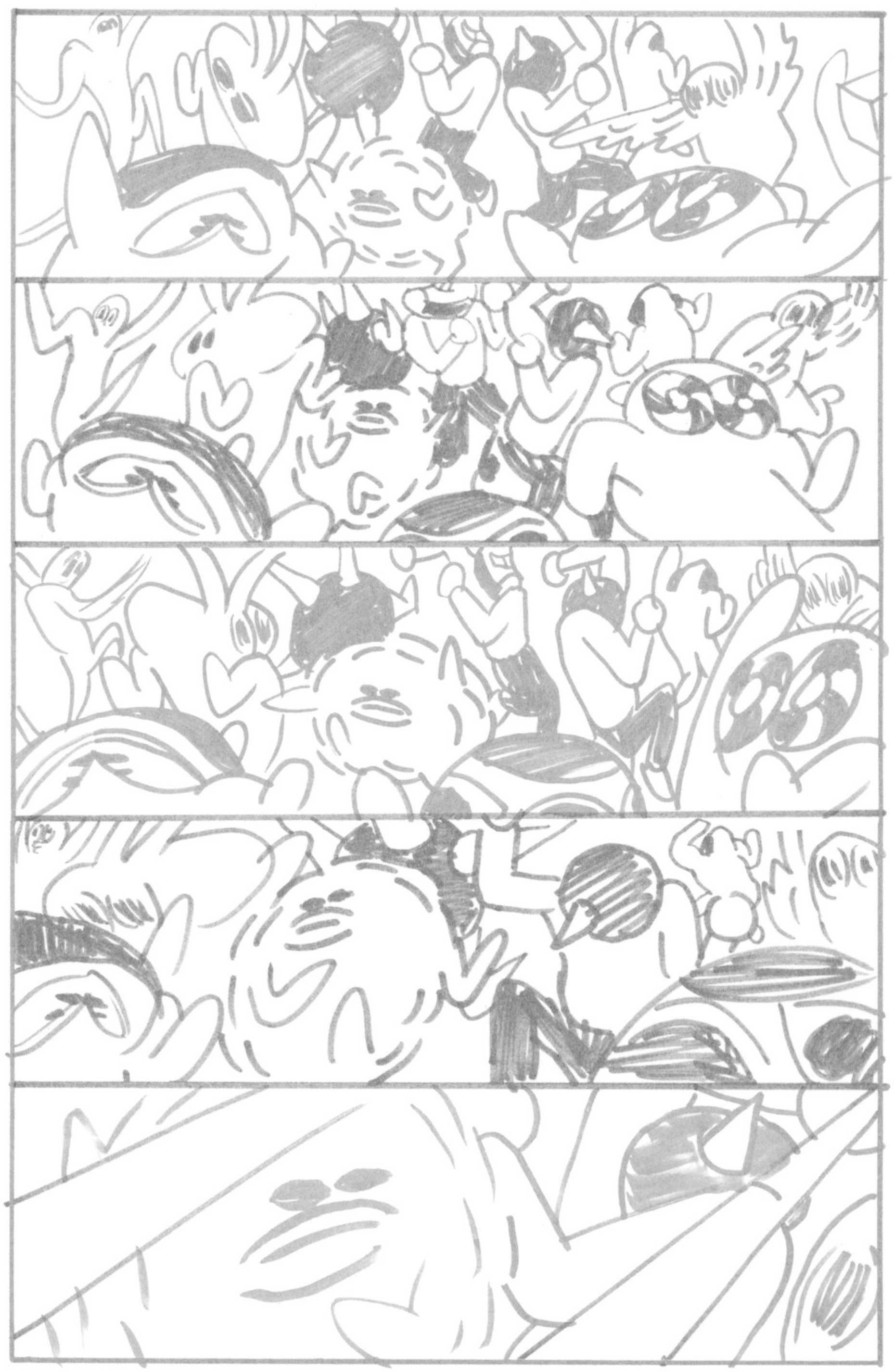

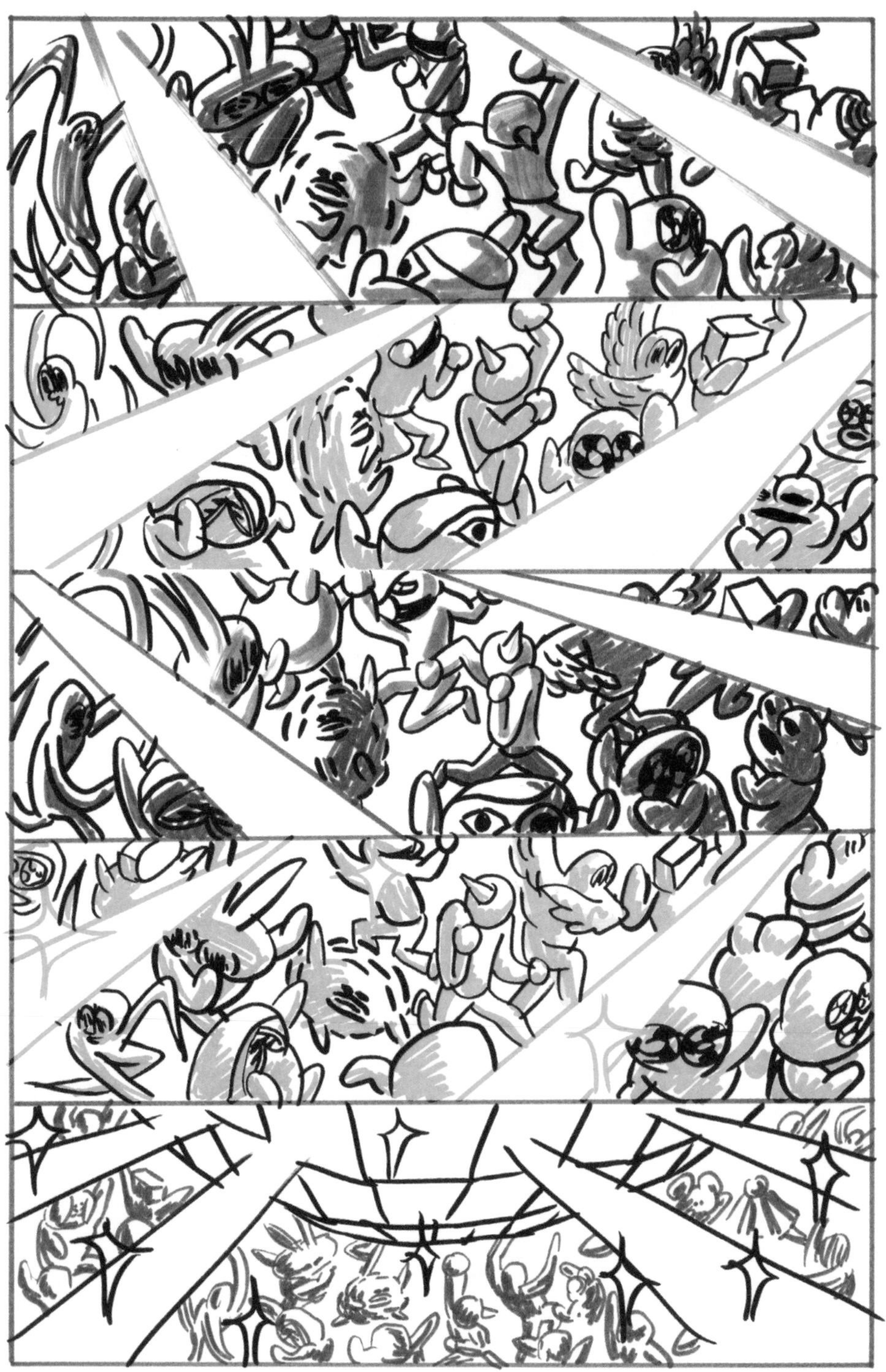

PFOOO
PFOOO
PFOOO
ZBLOOSH
SPLISH SPLISH
SPOP
SPLISH
SPLISH
SPLISH
SPLISH
BLOUF
VWOOM
WAAAA
WAAAA
BONG
WAAAA
WAAAA

WAAAA
SPLISH
SPLISH
SPLISH
SPLISH
WAAAA
SPLISH
SPLISH
SPLISH
WAAAA
WAAAA
SPLISH
SPLISH
SPLISH
SPLISH
WAAAA
WAAAA
SPLISH
SPLISH
SPLISH
SPLISH
WAAAA
WAAAA

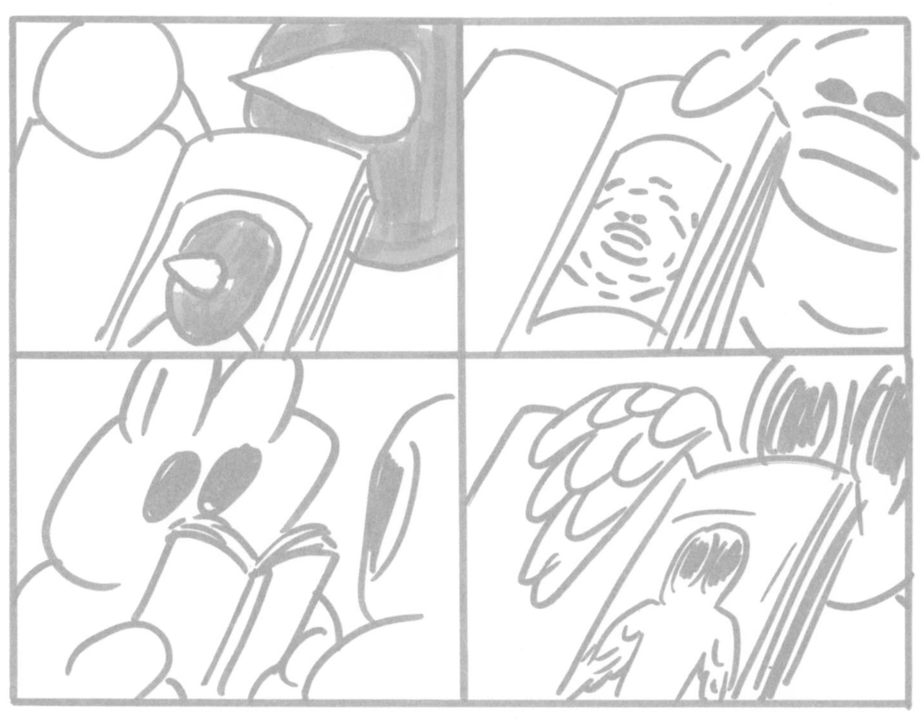

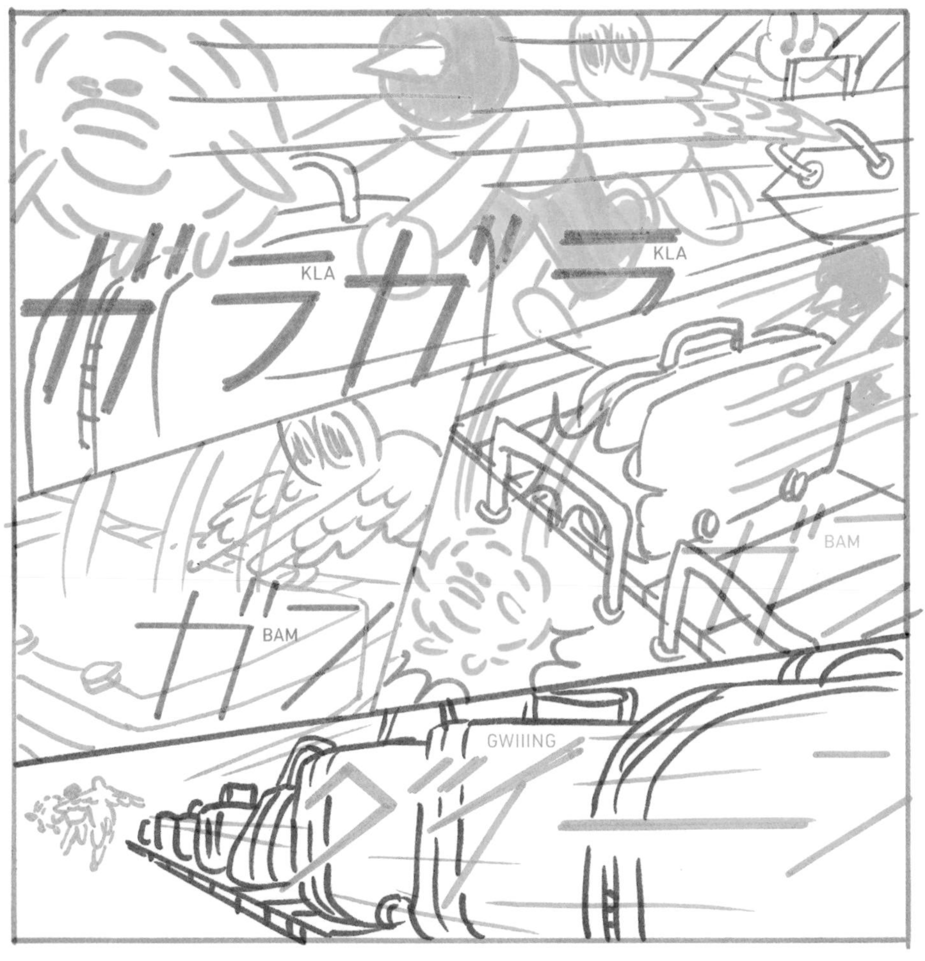
ガラガラ
KLA
KLA
BAM
ガ
BAM
GWIIING

TAP TAP TAP
TAP TAP TAP
TAP TAP TAP
GOOOOOO
BRRR BRRR
CLAC

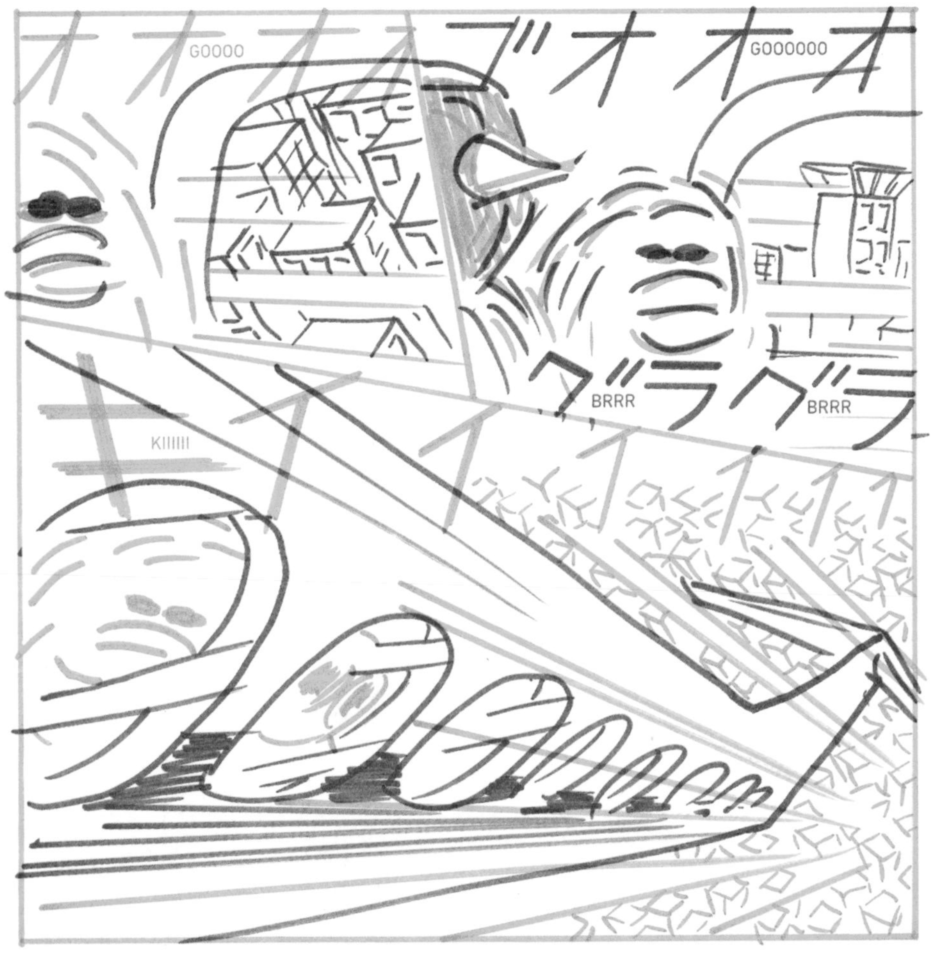
ゴオオオ
GOOOOOO
オオオオ
GOOOO
グラグラ
BRRR
BRRR
KIIIIII

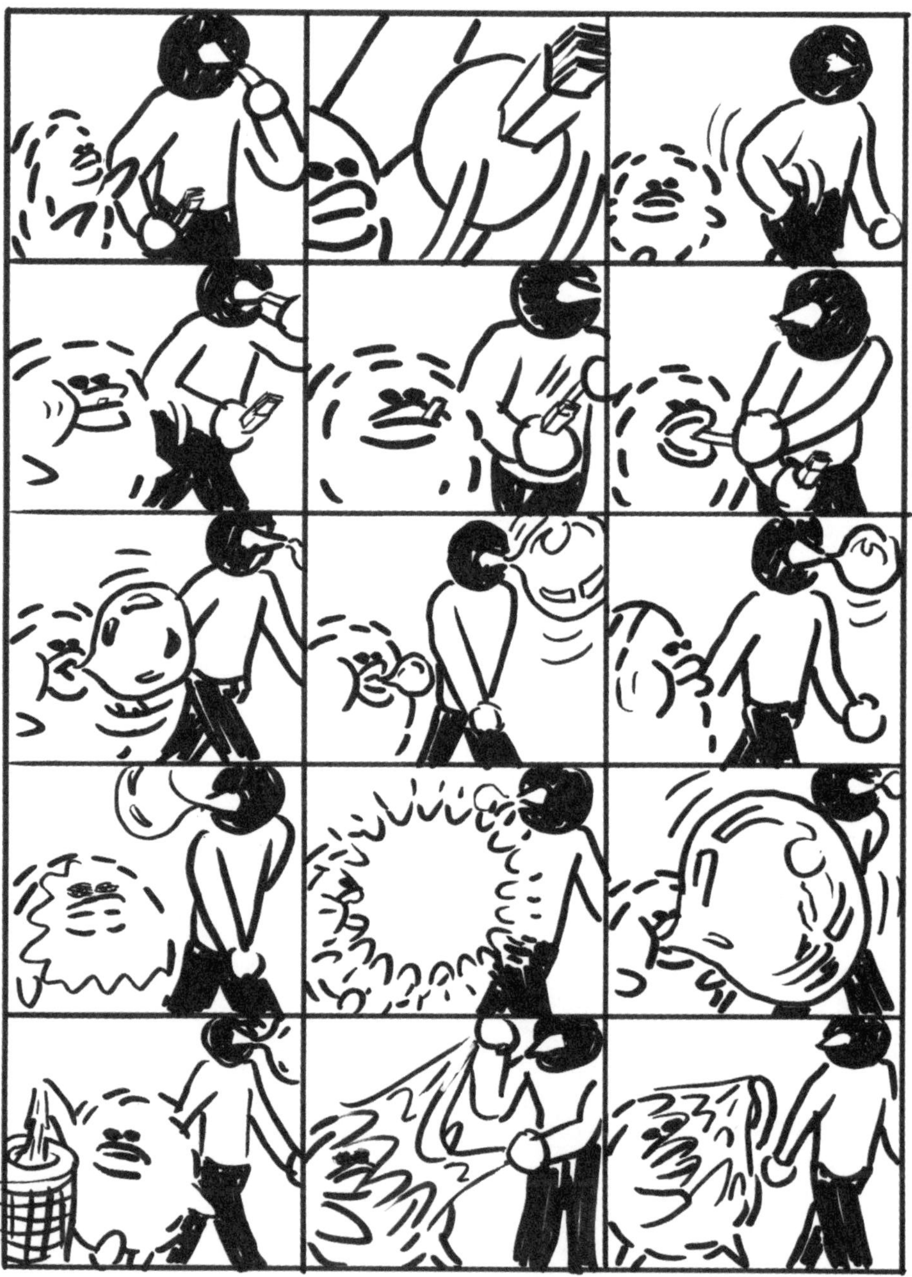

VWOOSH
VOUUUM
CLOK
WSSSSHH
WAAAA
TAP
TAP
TAP
WAAAA

BLOM
BLOM
TAP
TAP
TAP
TAP
TAP
TAP
VWOOM
BAF
WAAAA
TAP
TAP
TAP
WAAAA
BAH
SCHH
SCHH
BAH
WAAAA

POF
POF
ZAK
ZAK
PLAP
BLUP
BLUP
FLAK
FLAK
バラバラ
ZAK
ZAK
BLAP
PLOP
FRRI
FRRI
BAM
ガチャ
KCHIK
SHLURP
VRRRRR
FWUP
FWUP
FSCHHH

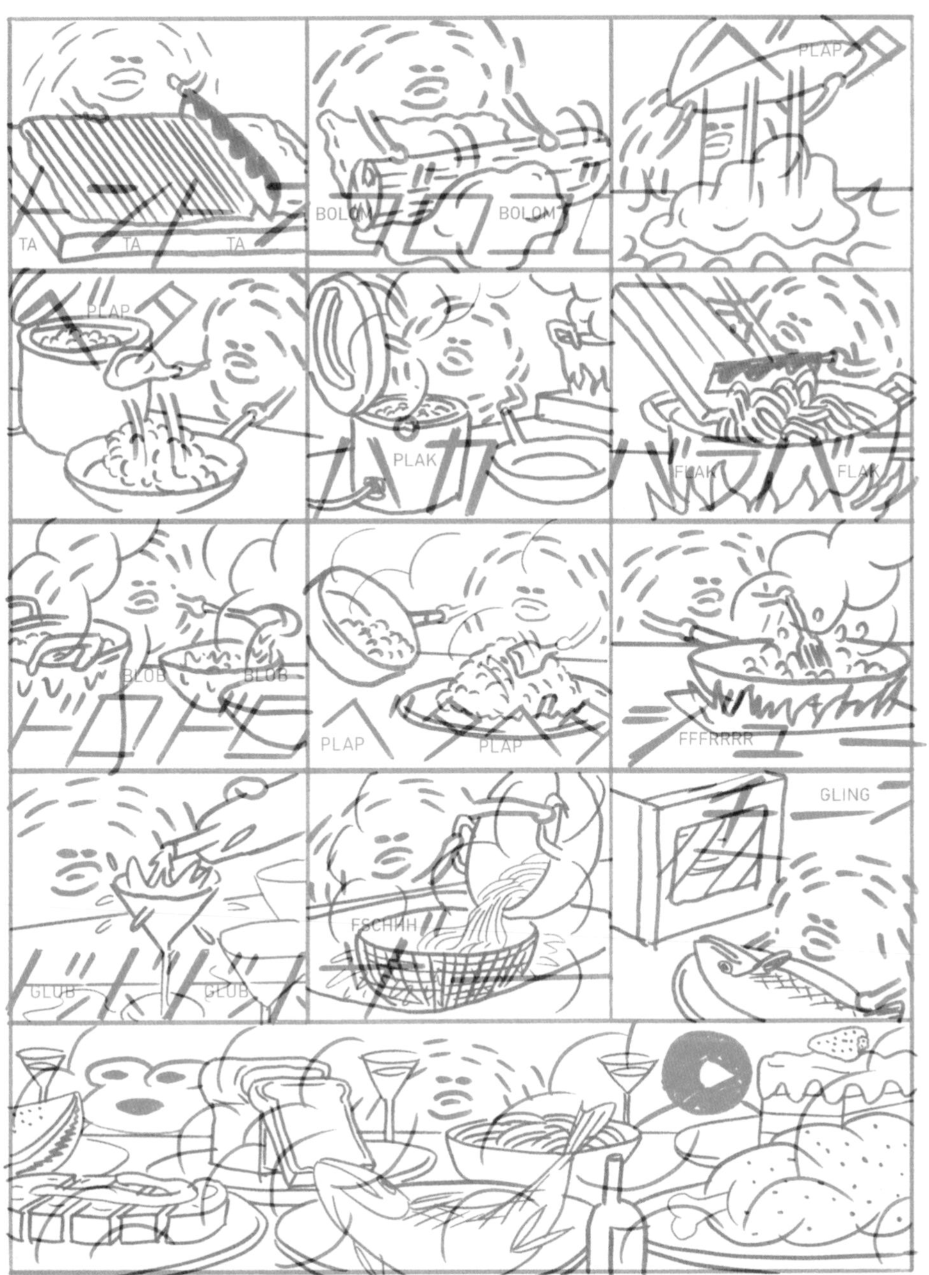
TA
TA
TA
BOLOM
BOLOM
PLAP
PLAP
PLAK
FLAK
FLAK
BLOB
BLOB
PLAP
PLAP
FFFRRRR
GLUB
GLUB
FSCHHH
GLING

CC

FWUP
FWUP
FWUP

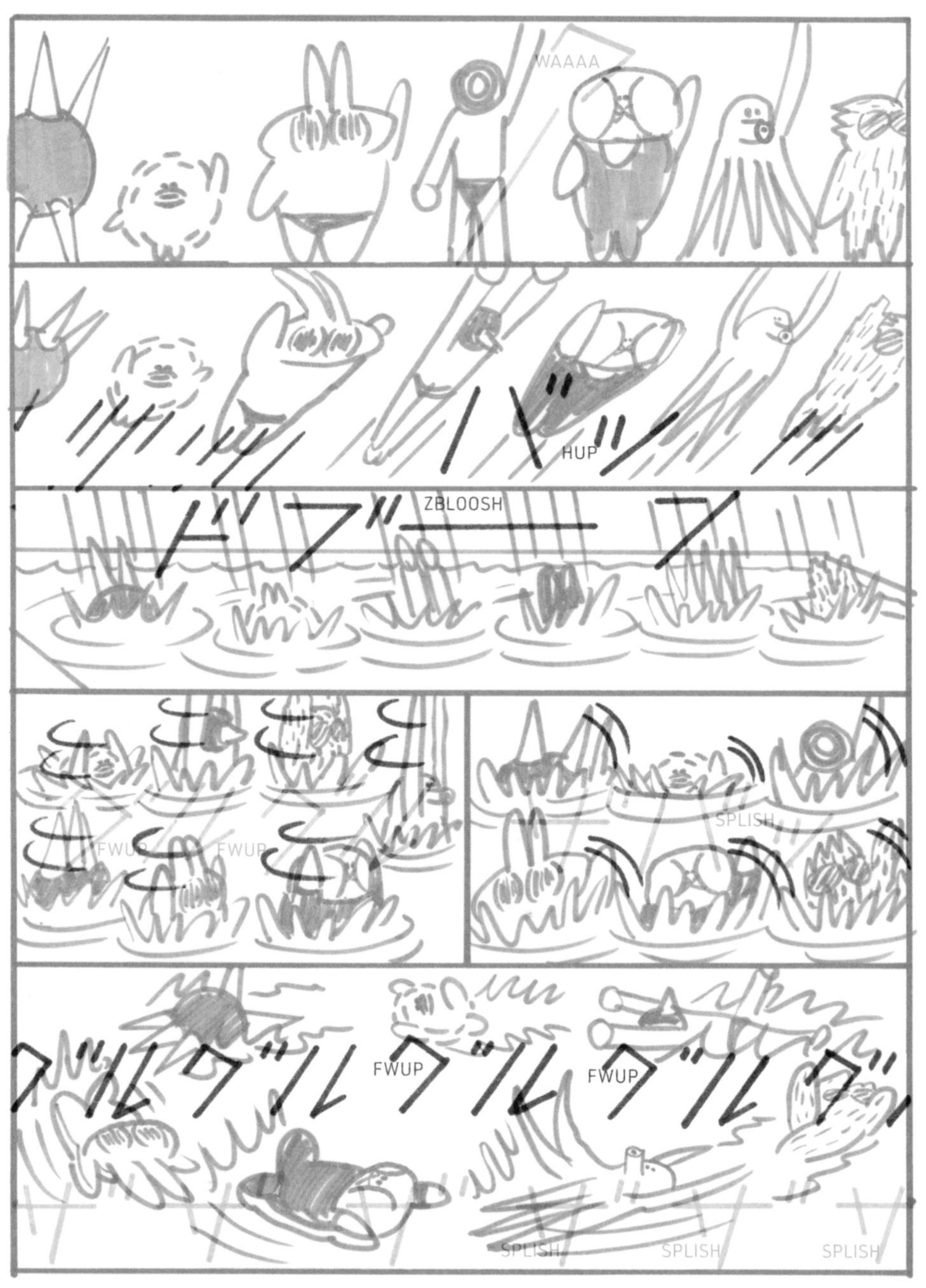
WAAAA
HUP
ZBLOOSH
FWUP
FWUP
SPLISH
FWUP
FWUP
SPLISH
SPLISH
SPLISH

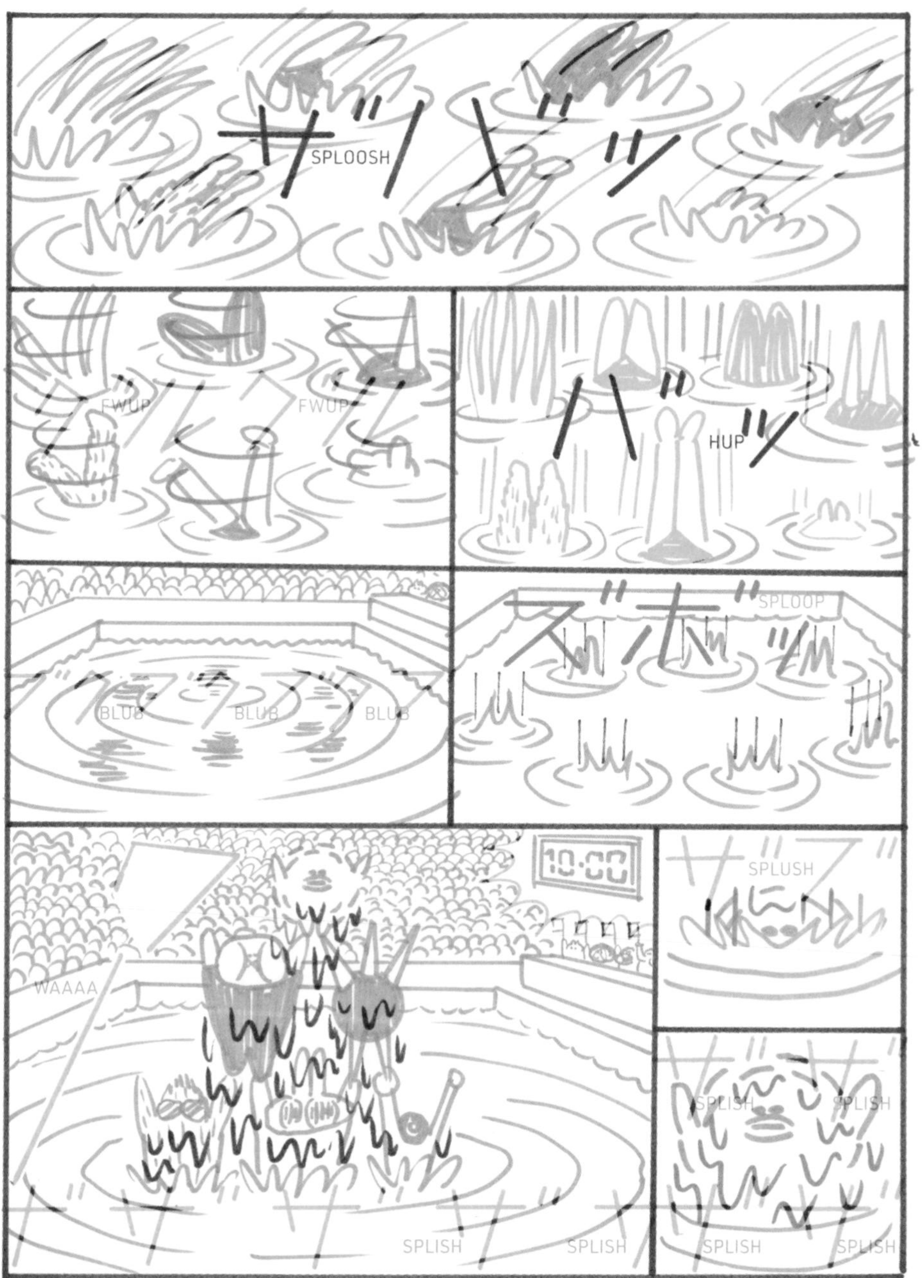
ザバッ
SPLOOSH
バッ
HUP
FWUP
FWUP
ズボボッ
SPLOOP
BLUB
BLUB
BLUB
SPLUSH
SPLISH
SPLISH
SPLISH
SPLISH
10:00
WAAAA
SPLISH
SPLISH

KWIIING

KWIIING

パチ
KCHIK
ザクザク
ZAK ZAK
ザクザク
ZAK ZAK
ザクザク
ZAK ZAK
ザク
ZAK
ザク
ZAK

ザ゛ー
FSCHHH
ザ゛ー
FSCHHH
ザ゛ー
FSCHHH
ザ゛ー
FSCHHH
ザ゛ー
FSCHHH
ザ゛ー
FSCHHH
ザ゛ー
FSCHHH
ザ゛ー
FSCHHH
ザ゛ー
FSCHHH
ザ゛ー
FSCHHH
ザ゛ー
FSCHHH
ザ゛ー
ザ゛ー
FSCHHH
ザ゛ー
FSCHHH

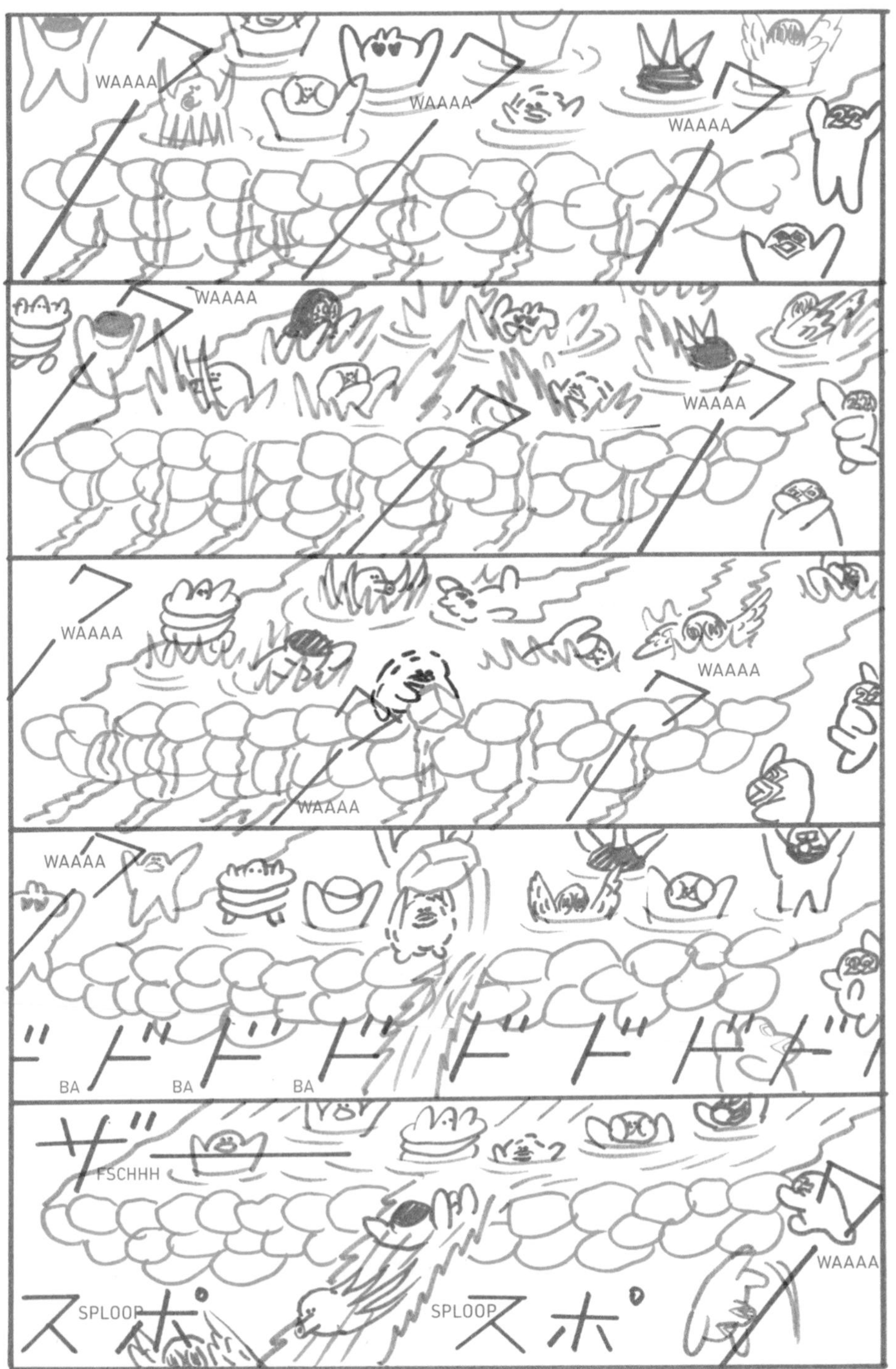
WAAAA
WAAAA
WAAAA
WAAAA
WAAAA
WAAAA
WAAAA
WAAAA
WAAAA
ドドドドドドド
BA
BA
BA
ザー
FSCHHH
WAAAA
スポ
SPLOOP
スポ
SPLOOP

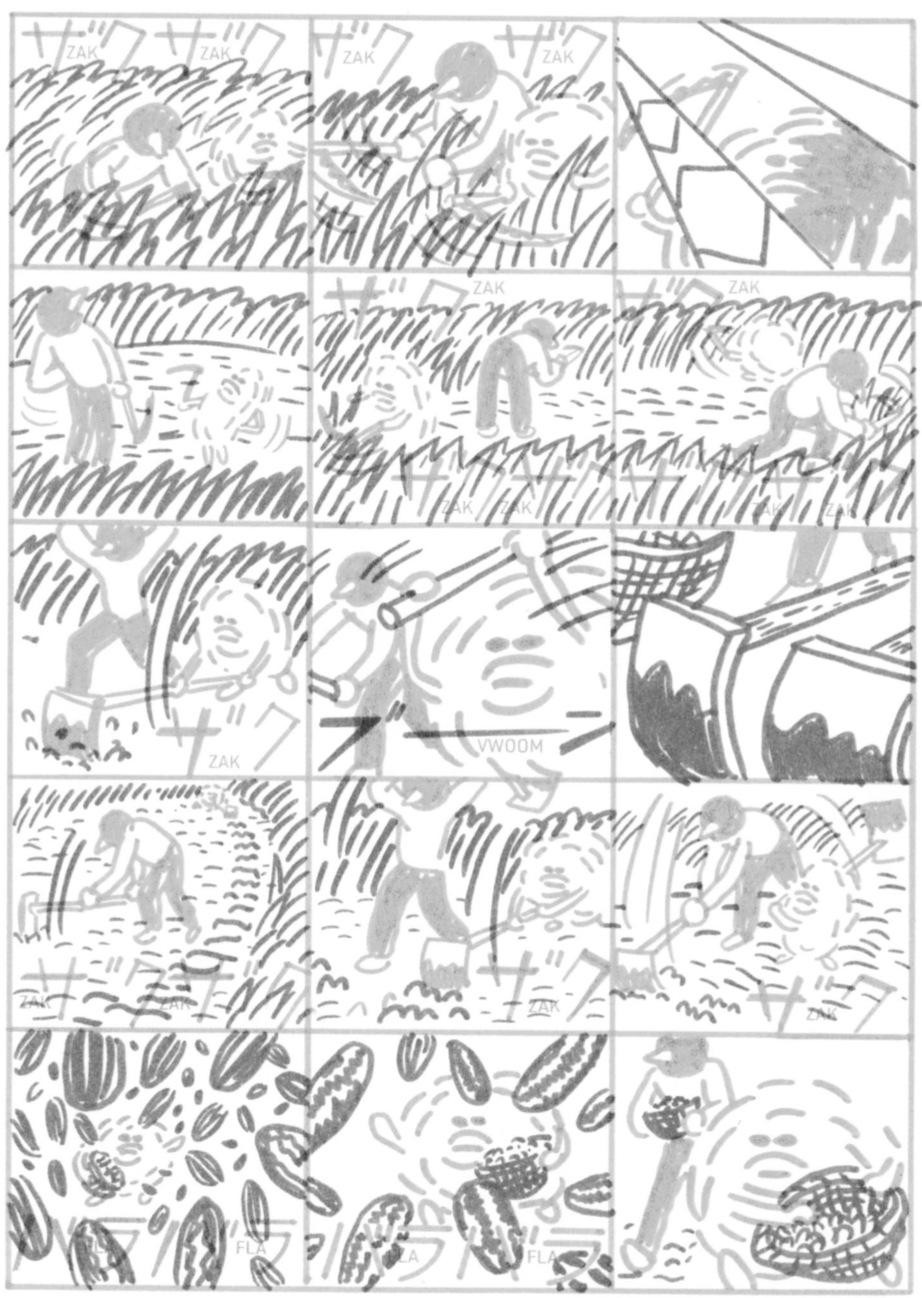
ザク
ZAK
ザク
ZAK
ザク
ZAK
ザク
ZAK
ザク
ZAK
ZAK
ZAK
ZAK
ZAK
ZAK
ザク
ZAK
VWOOM
ZAK
ZAK
ザク
ZAK
ザク
ZAK
FLA
FLA
FLA
FLA

SPLOOSH
SPLOOSH
FLA
FLA
DOF
SPLOOSH
SPLOOSH
SPLOOSH
TAP TAP TAP
TAP TAP TAP
TAP TAP TAP
TAP TAP TAP

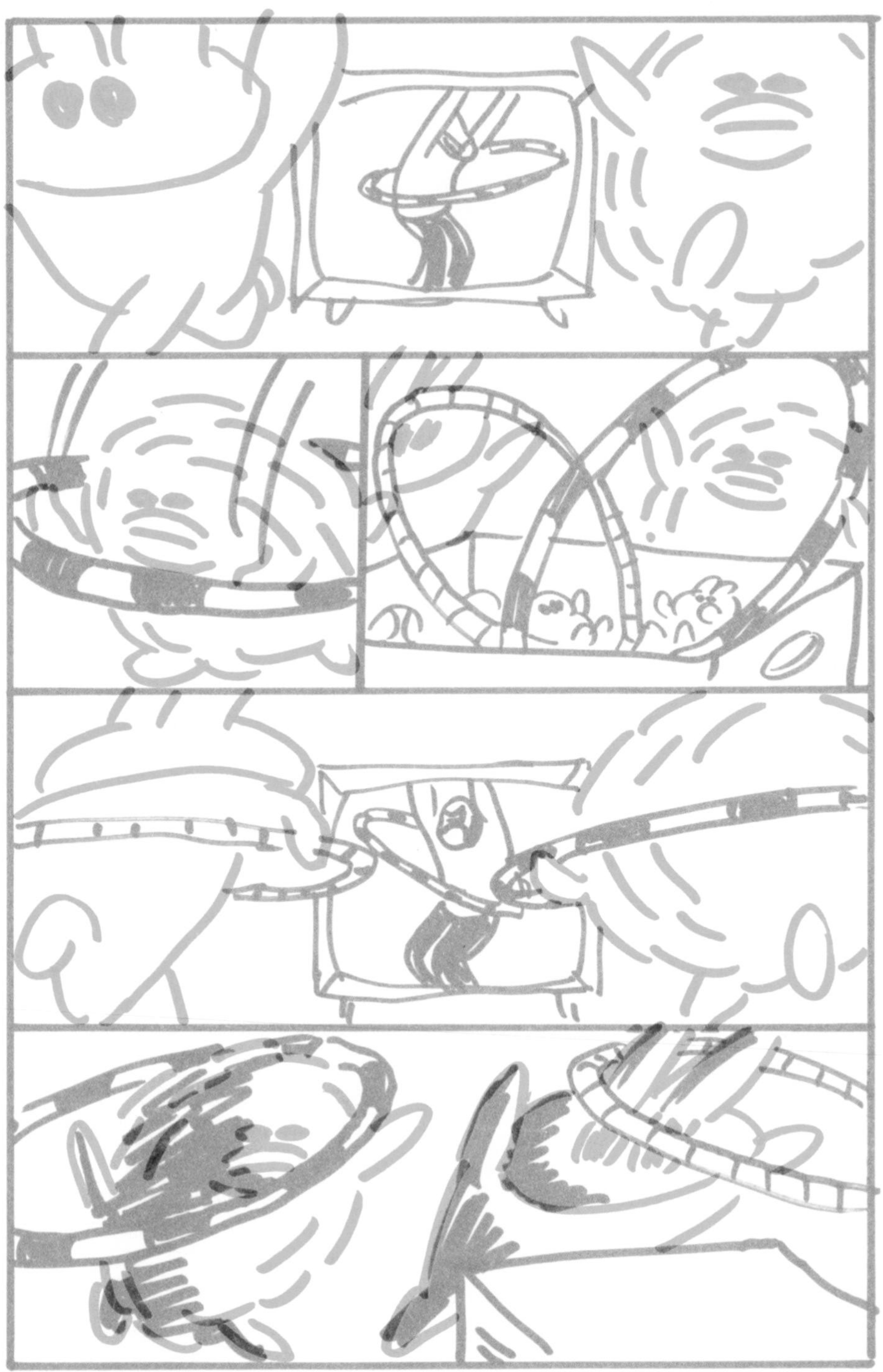

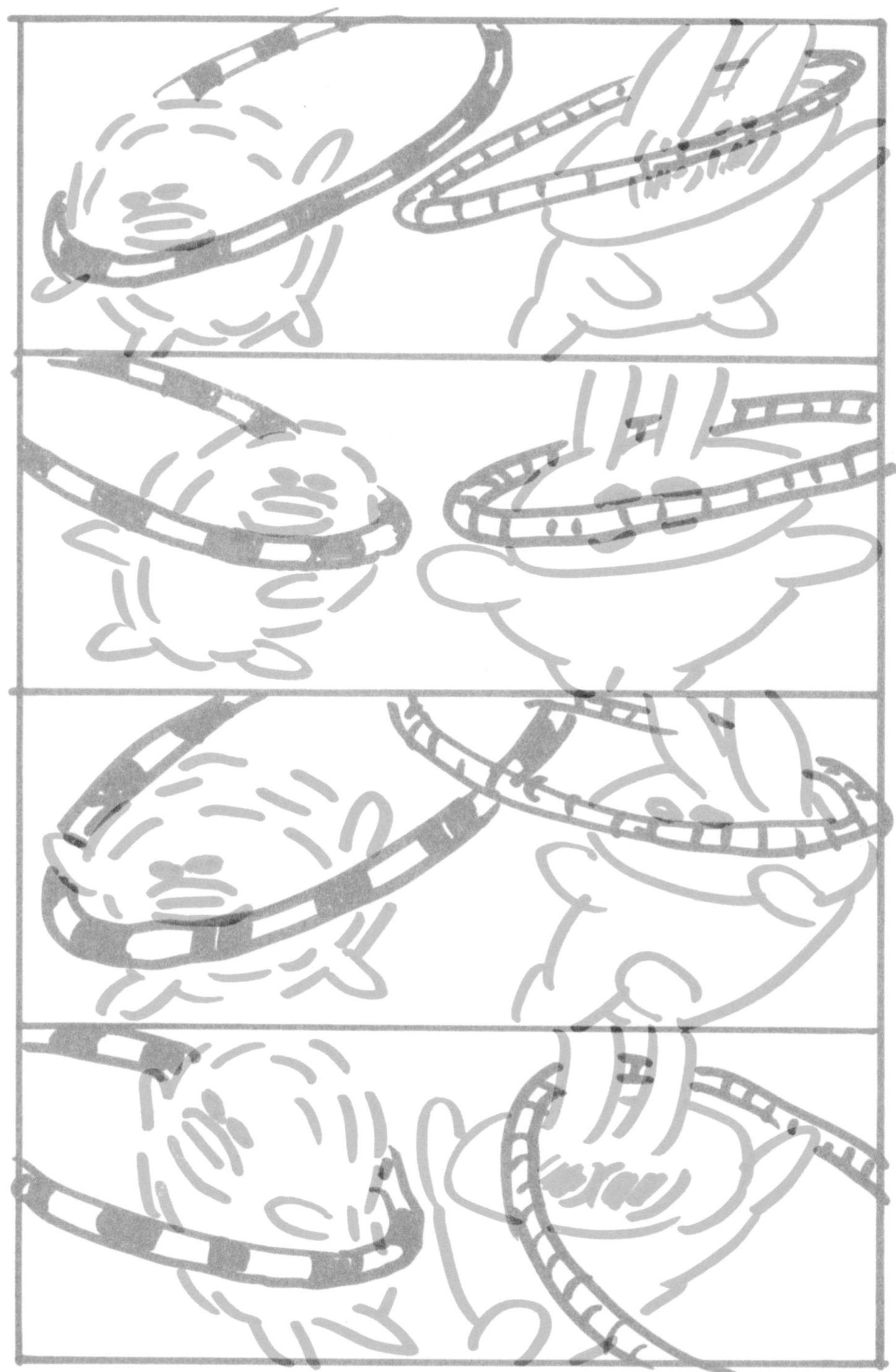

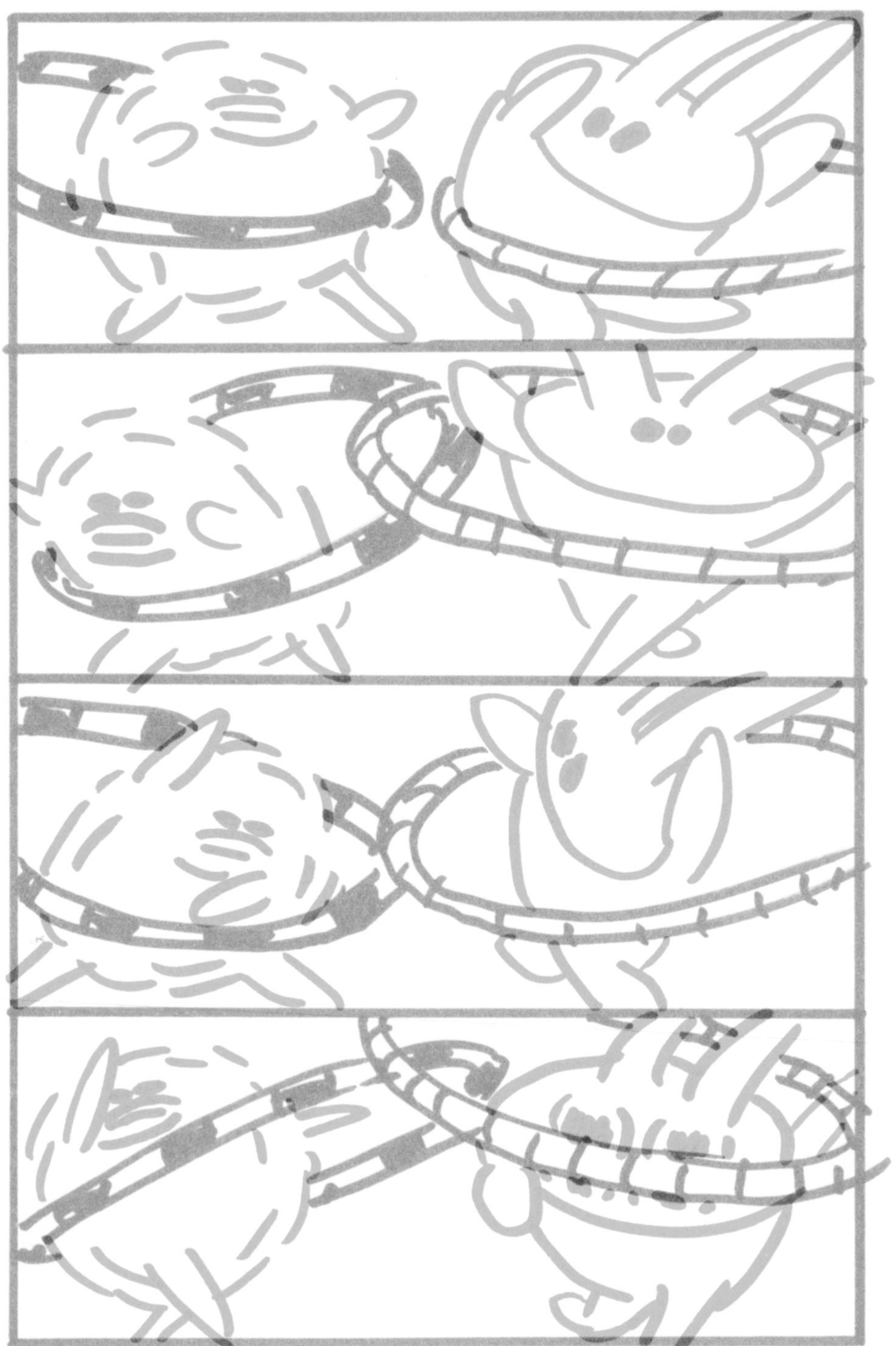

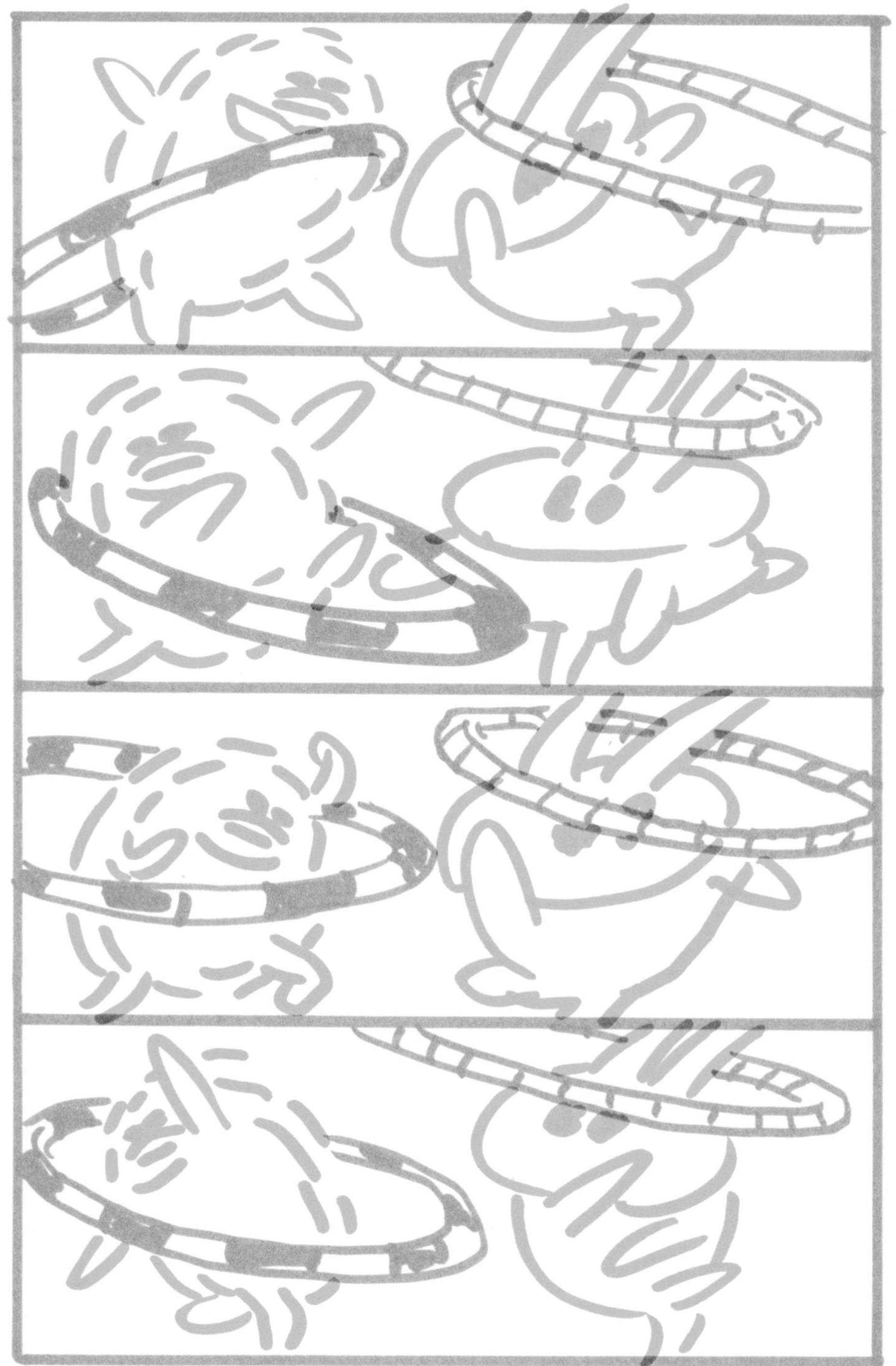

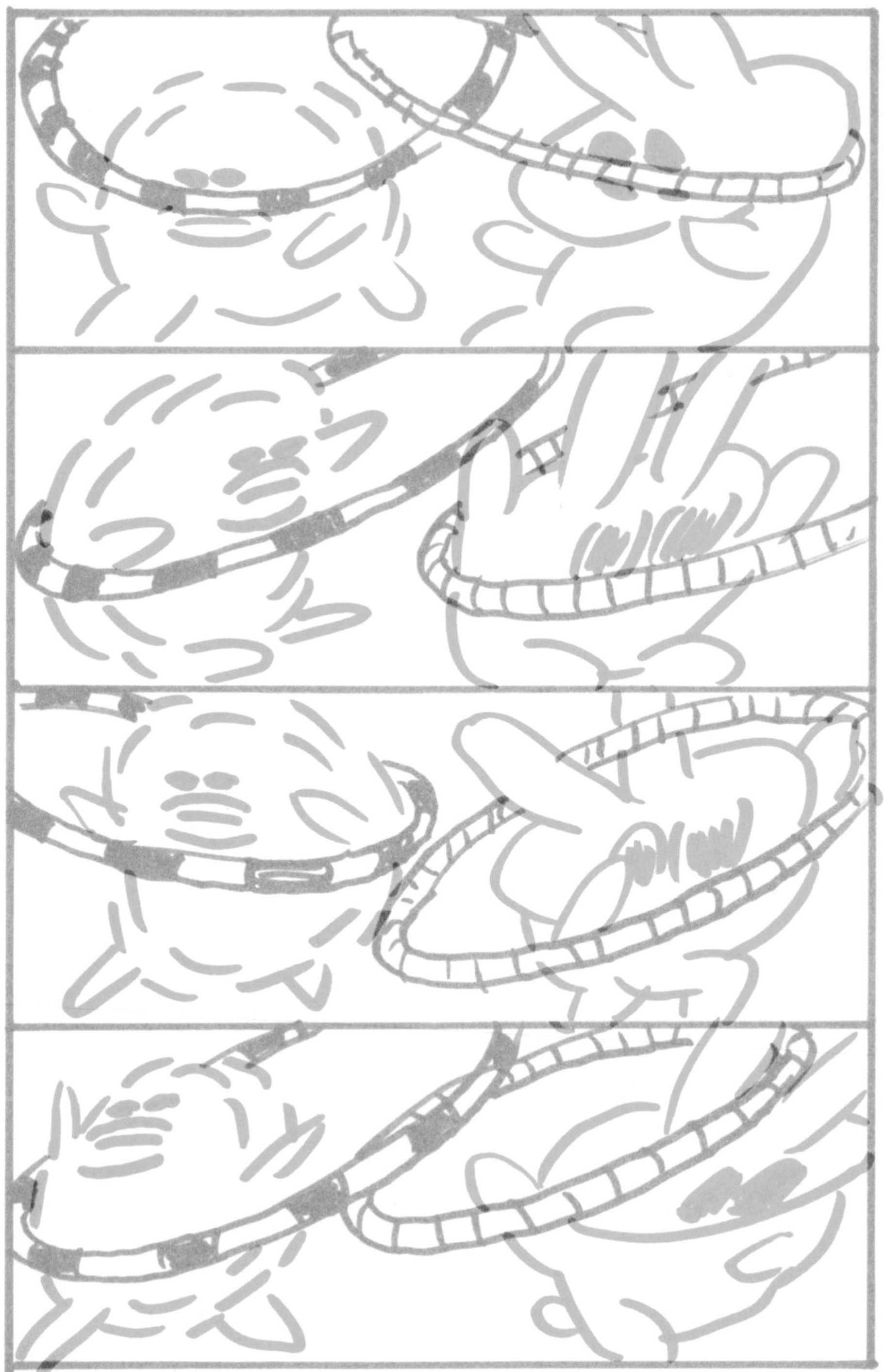

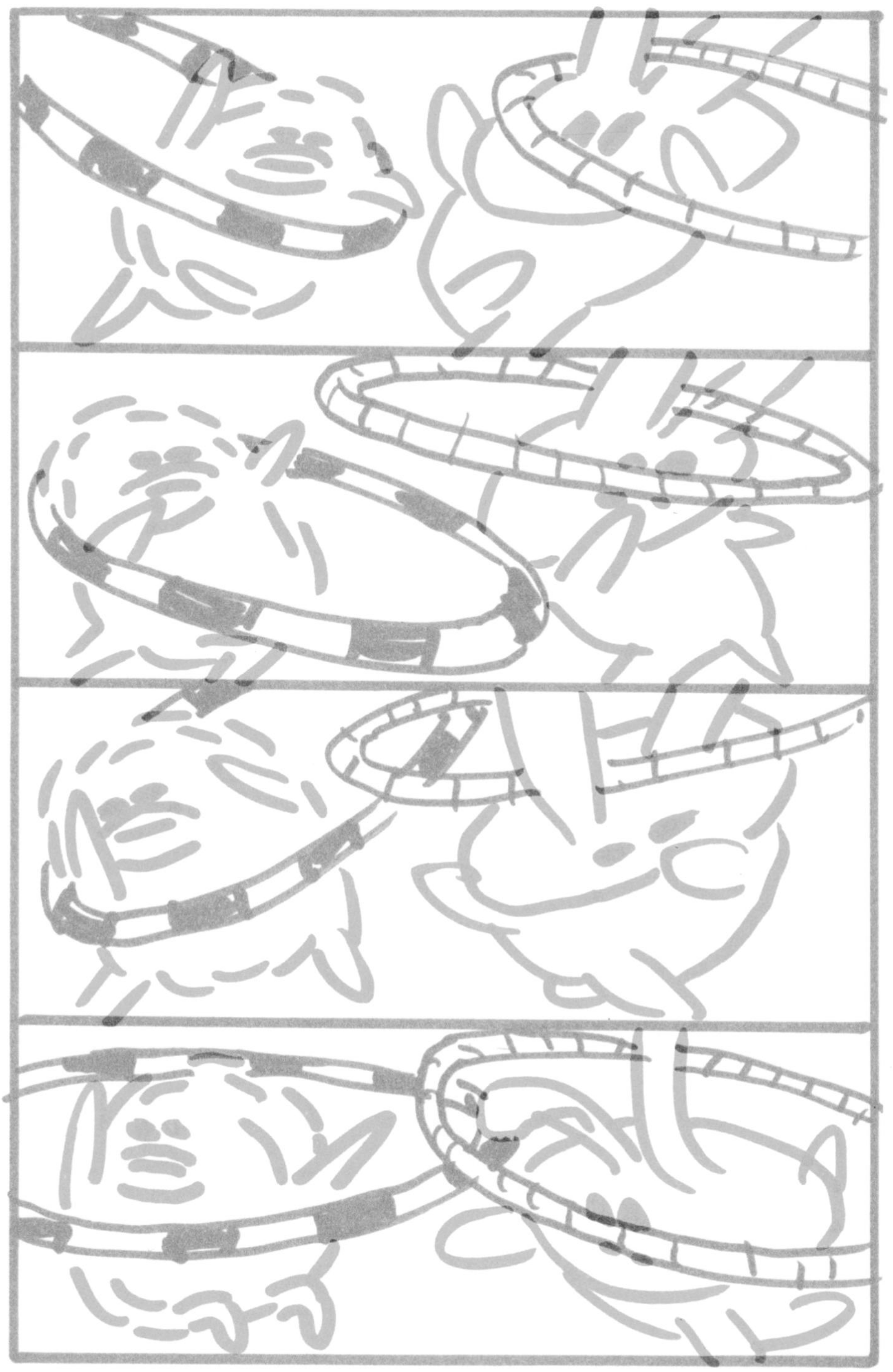

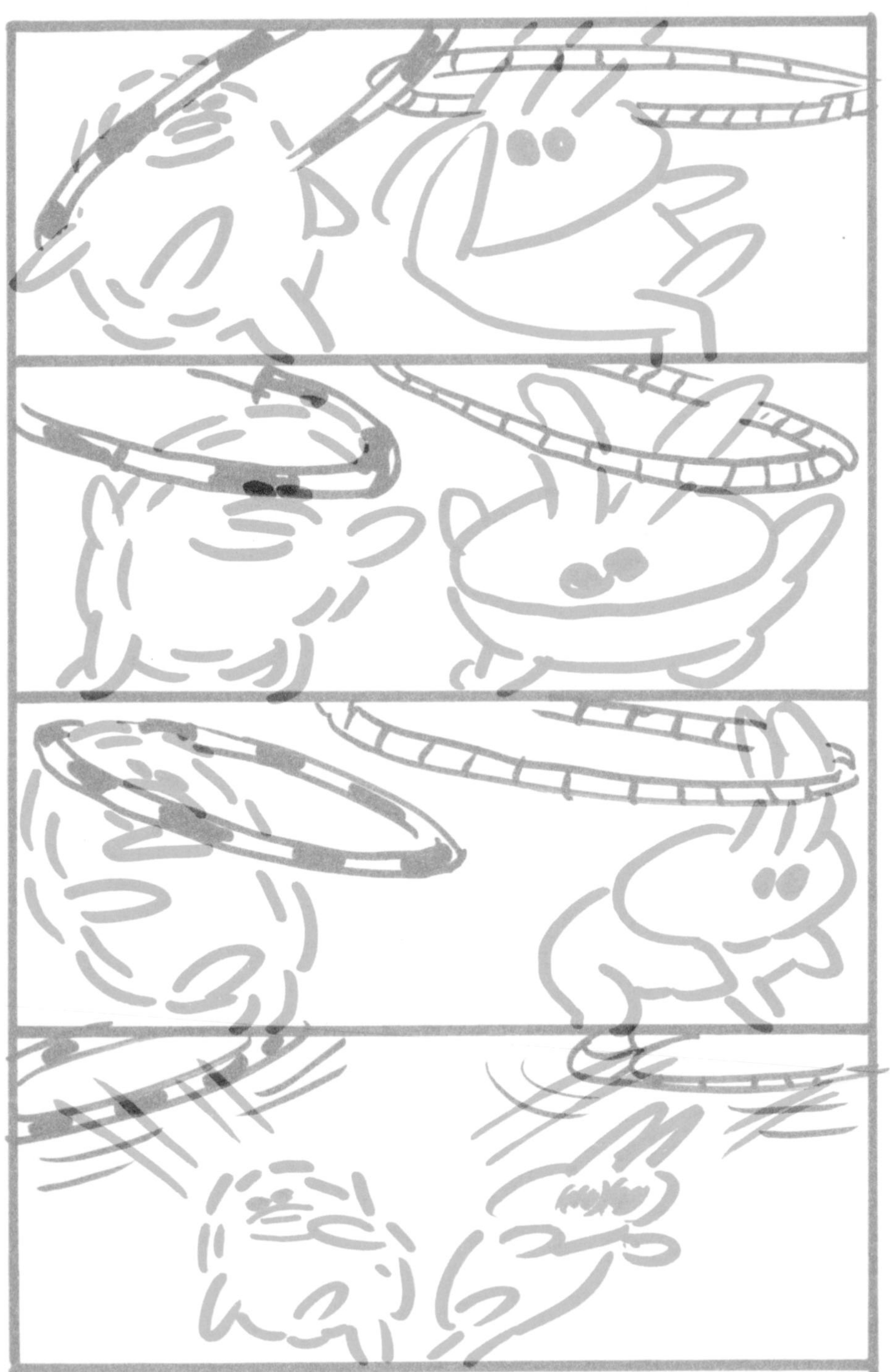

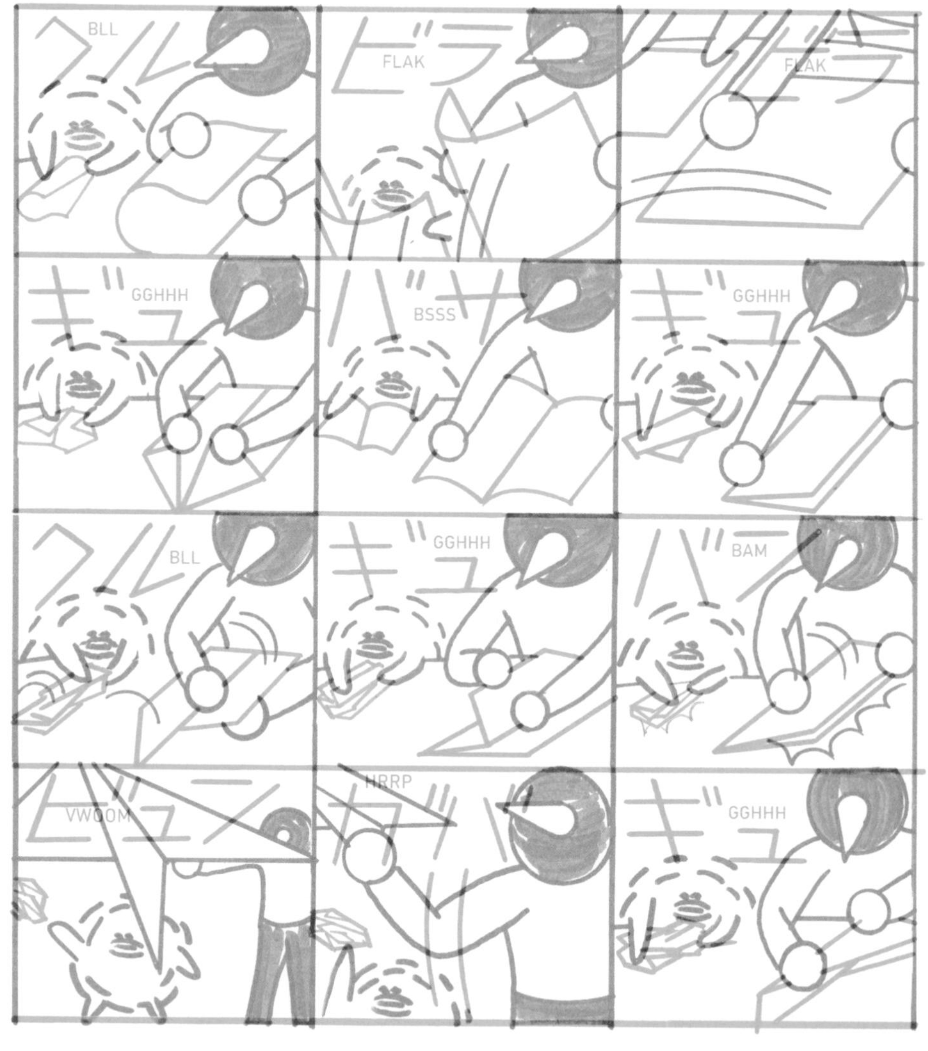
BLL
FLAK
FLAK
GGHHH
BSSS
GGHHH
BLL
GGHHH
BAM
VWOOM
HRRP
GGHHH

BR
BR
BR
BR
BR
BR
BR
BR
BOM
BLOM
BLOM
BLOM
BR
BR

WAAAA
BLOM
BLOM
BLOM
BLOM
BLOM
BLOM
BLOM
WAAAA
BLUB
BLUB
BLOM
BLOM
BLOM
WAAAA
DONG
DONG
BLOM
BLOM
BLOM
WAAAA
BLOM
BLOM
WAAAA

WAAAA
WAAAA
WAAAA
WAAAA
TAP
TAP
TAP
TAP

WAAAA
TAP
TAP
TAP
TAP
TAP
TAP
WAAAA
TAP
TAP
TAP
TAP
WAAAA
WAAAA
BOING
BOING
BOING
WAAAA
WAAAA
WAAAA
BOING
WAAAA
BOING
TAP
TAP
TAP

WAAAA
WAAAA
BOING
BOING
BOING
BOING
BOING
BOING
BOING
BOING
BOING
BOING
BOING
WAAAA
WAAAA

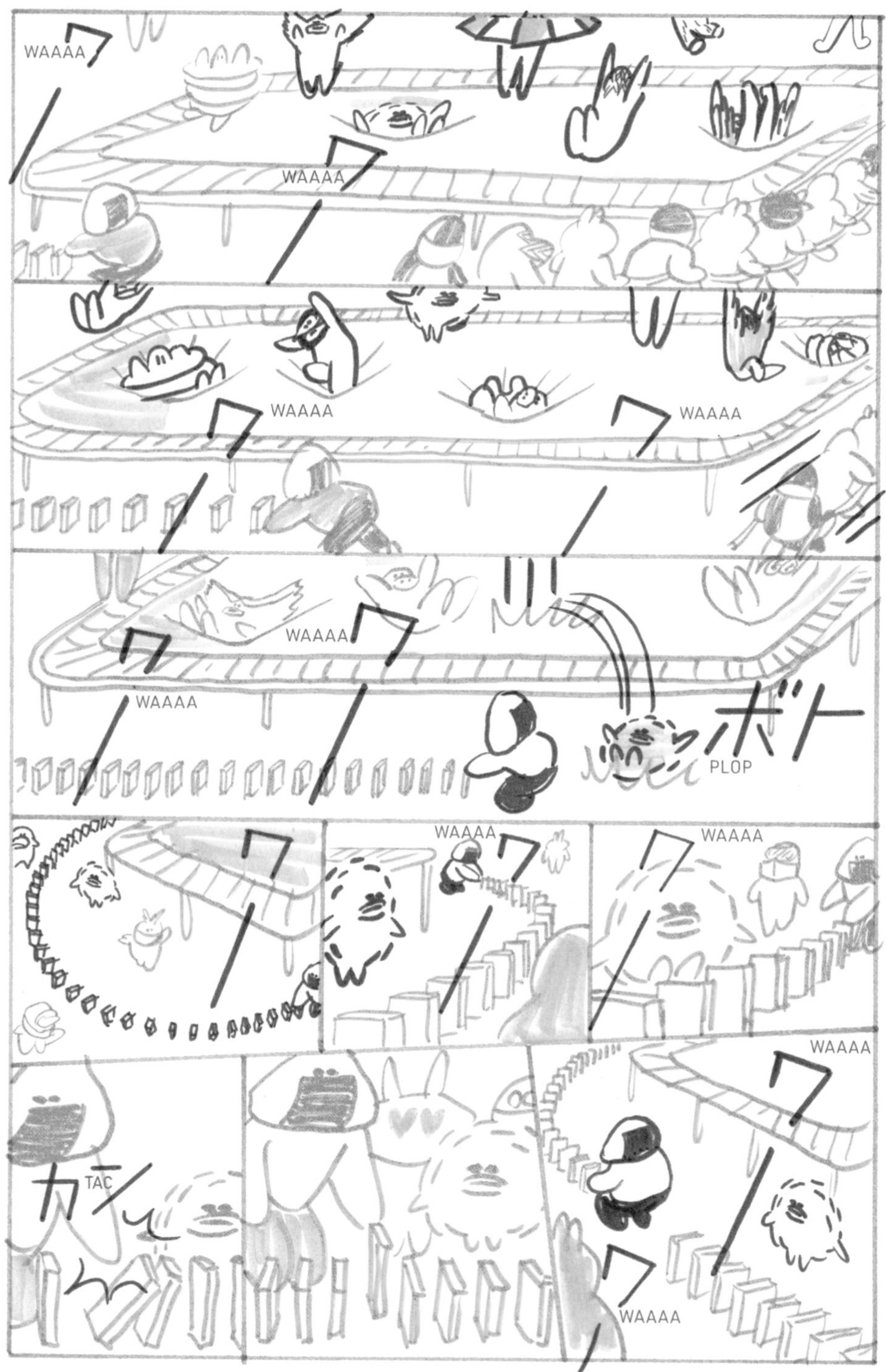

WAAAA
ワ
WAAAA
ワ
WAAAA
ワ
WAAAA
ワ
WAAAA
ワ
WAAAA
ワ
ボト
PLOP
WAAAA
ワ
WAAAA
ワ
WAAAA
ワ
カン
TAC
WAAAA
ワ
WAAAA
ワ

PLAK
PLAK
パタパタ
WAAAA
PLAK
PLAK
パタパタ
パタパタ
PLAK
PLAK
WAAAA
WAAAA
パタパタ
PLAK
PLAK
WAAAA
パタパタ
WAAAA
パタパタ
PLAK
PLAK
BOING
BOING
WAAAA
PLAK
PLAK
パタパタ
FWUP
FWUP
クルクル
FWUP
FWUP
WAAAA
FWUP
FWUP
クルクル
FWUP
FWUP

WAAAA
WAAAA
FWUP
FWUP
WAAAA
FWUP
FWUP
FLAP
FLAP
FLAP
FWUP
FWUP
FWUP
FWUP
TAP
TAP
TAP
TAP
BOOOHH
WAAAA
TAP
TAP
TAP
TAP
WAAAA
TAP
TAP
TAP
TAP

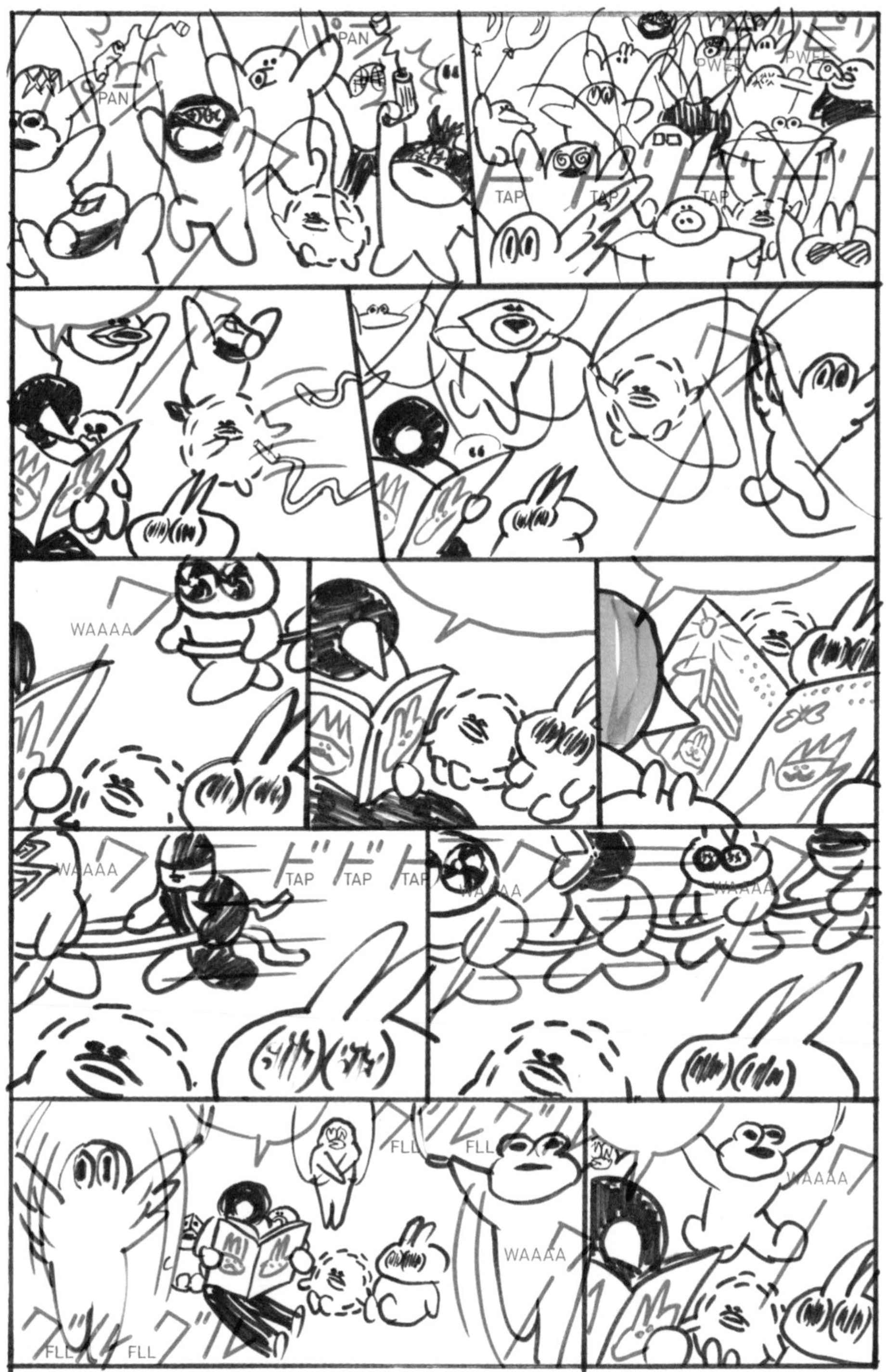

PAN
PAN
PWEE
PWEE
TAP
TAP
TAP
WAAAA
WAAAA
TAP
TAP
TAP
WAAAA
WAAAA
FLL
FLL
WAAAA
FLL
FLL
WAAAA

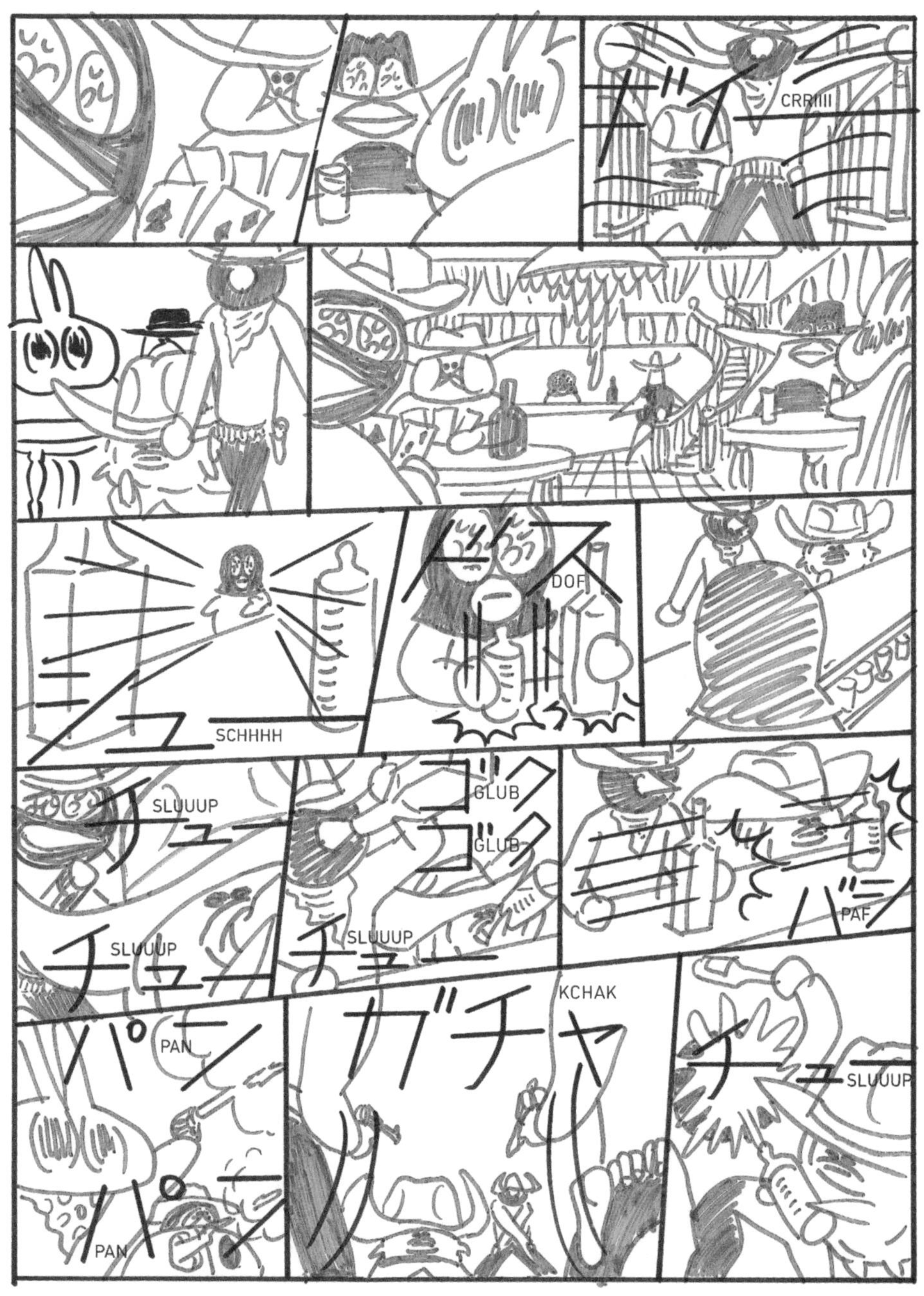

CRRIIII
SCHHHH
DOF
SLUUUP
GLUB
GLUB
SLUUUP
SLUUUP
PAF
PAN
PAN
KCHAK
SLUUUP

KAPOW
KAPOW
KCKAK
KLISH
BISH
BANG
WAAAA
PAN
PAN
TAP
TAP
TAP
TAP
TAP
TAP
KLAASH
SNAP
POF
POF
SWISH
POW
POW

HRRP
ZBLOOSH
BLUB
BLUB
BLUB
BLUB
BLUB
BLUB
FLASH
BLUB
BLUB
BLUB
FLASH
BAH
STOOMP
FLAP
FLAP
FLAP

カラャ
FLASH
シュッ
SHWUP
モクモク
PUF
PUF
モクモク
PUF
PUF
モクモクモク
PUF
PUF
PLAC
パカ
PFFF
チューー
NWOOP
ニュー
CRR
CRR
スルスル
CRR
CRR
スルスル
CRR
CRR

FLAP
FLAP
WAAAA
FLL
FLL
FLL
FLA
FLA
PSCHIII
WAAAA
WAAAA
WAAAA
WAAAA
WAAAA
PAF
SHLING
FLASH
WAAAA
PWEEW
WAAAA

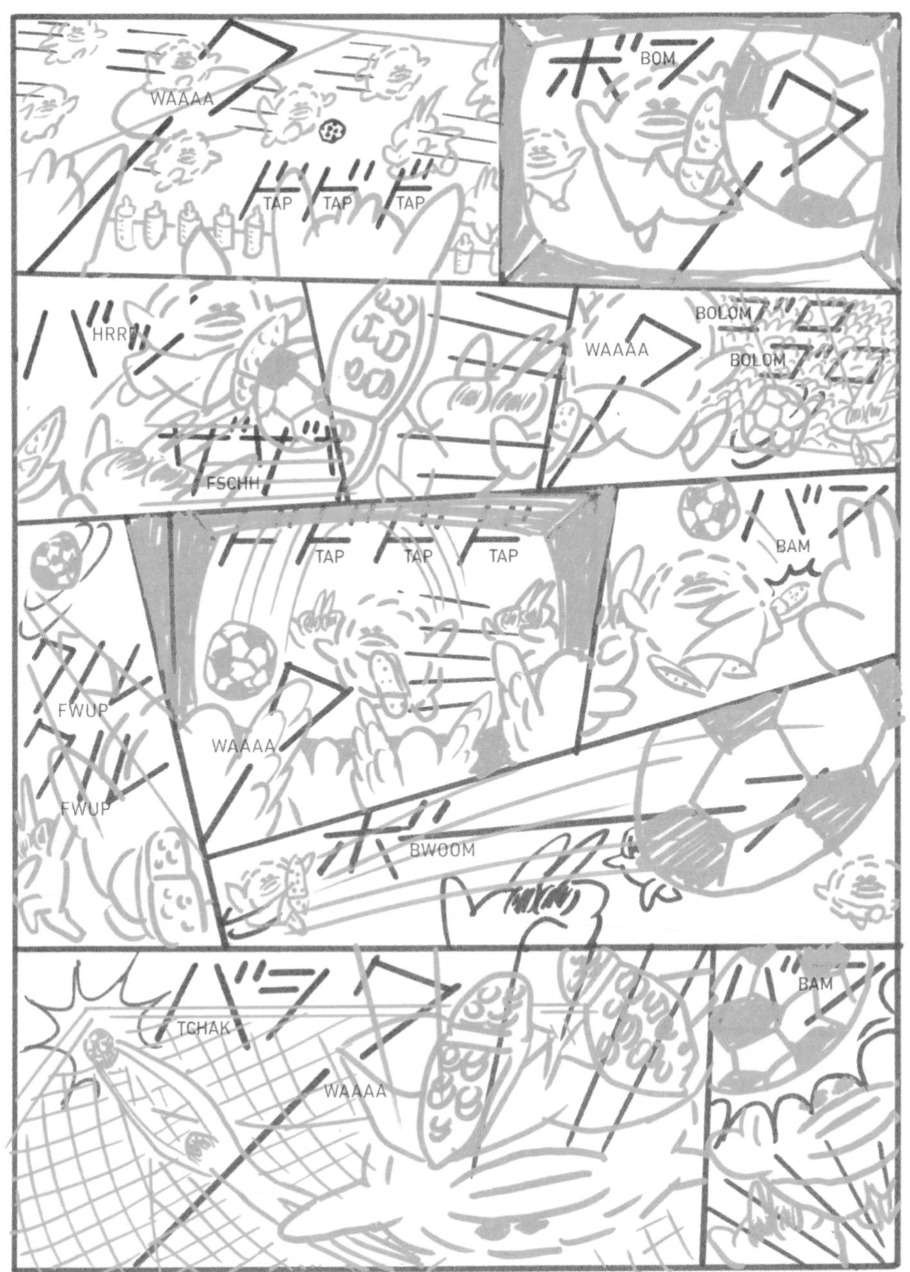
BOM
WAAAA
TAP TAP TAP
BOLOM
BOLOM
WAAAA
FSCHH
BAM
TAP TAP TAP
WAAAA
FWUP
FWUP
BWOOM
BAM
TCHAK
WAAAA

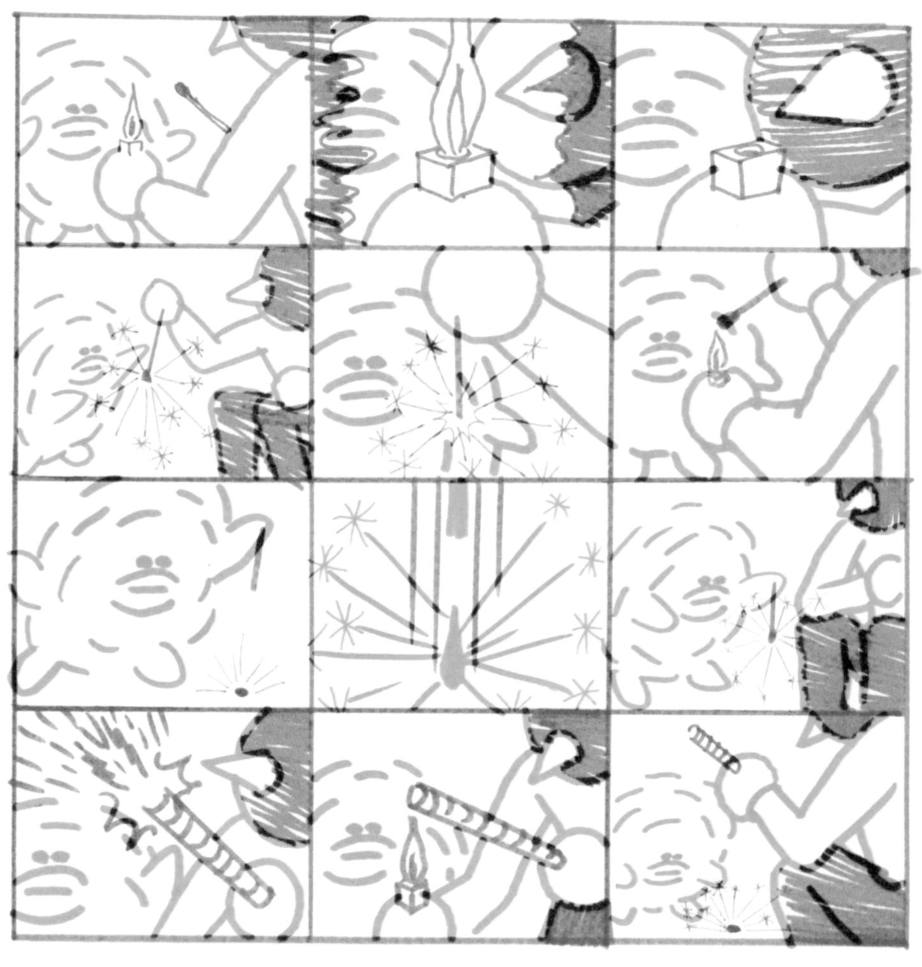

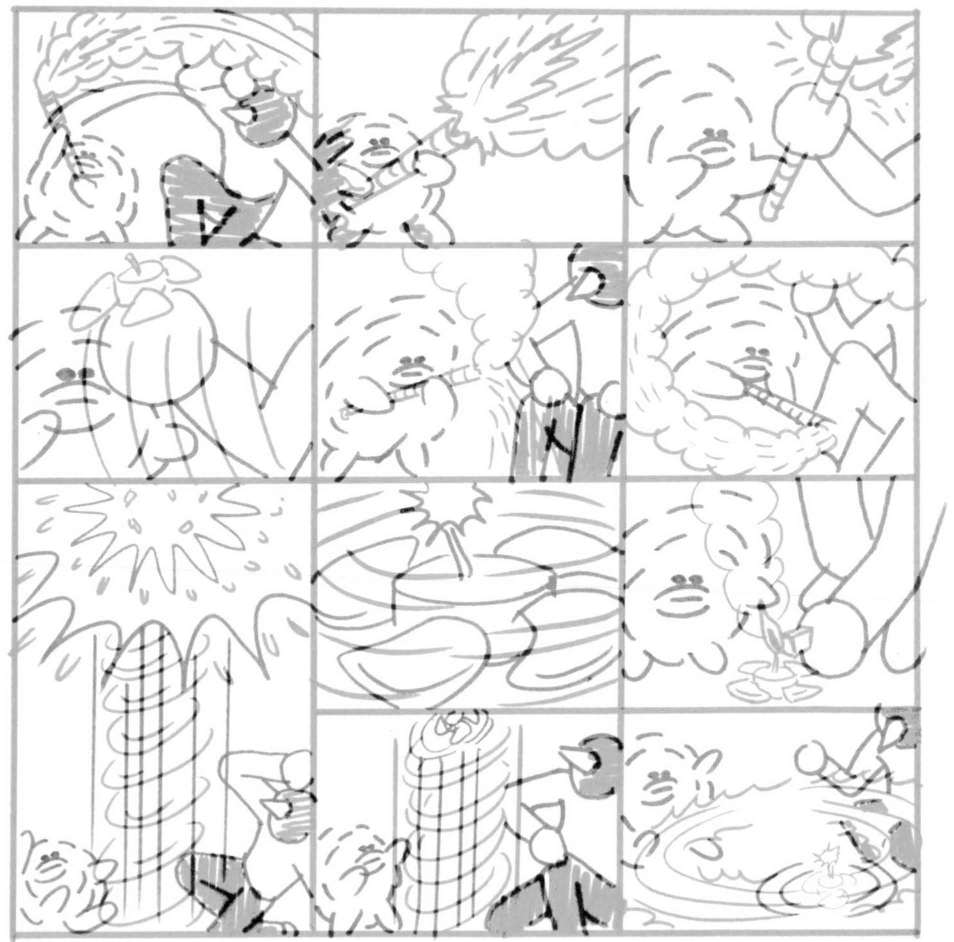

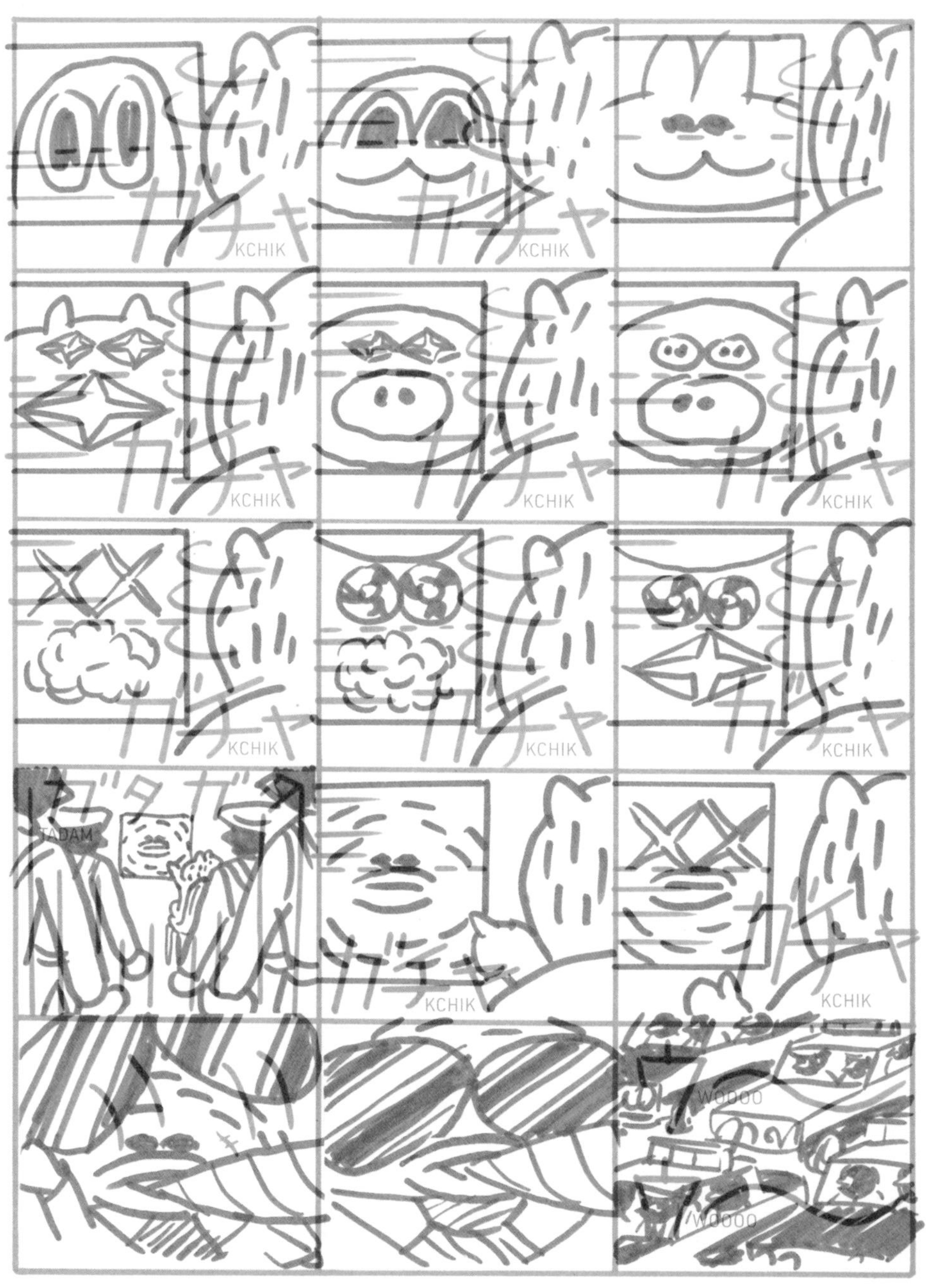

KCHIK
KCHIK
ガチャ
KCHIK
ガチャ
KCHIK
ガチャ
KCHIK
ガチャ
KCHIK
ガチャ
KCHIK
ガチャ
KCHIK
TADAM
ガチャ
KCHIK
ガチャ
KCHIK
WOOOO
WOOOO

CLIC
KCHIK
WOOOO
UUUUHH
KWIIING
BAM
KCHIK
WAAAA
WAAAA
TAP
TAP
TAP
CLANG
CLANG
KCHIK

カチ
CLAC
SHLING
FWUP
PAK
PAK
CLING
BAH
CLING
HRRP
CLANG
VWOOM

WAAAA
TAP
TAP
TAP
TAP
TAP
TAP
WAAAA
SPAH
SPAH
SPAH
SPAH
TCHAC
SCHLL
SCHLL
TAC
TAC
TAC
WAAAA
TAP
TAP
TAP
WAAAA
WAAAA
TAP
TAP
TAP
TAP

グイーン
GWIIING
パカ
PLAC
スポ
SPOP
スポ
SPOP
パカ
PLAC
パカ
PLAC
ガチャ
KCHANG
グイーー

Portions of *Baby Boom* might be seen as a "comics of attractions," where what the reader enjoys most is not reminders of daily life per se, but rather their representation in the medium of comics. The inventive graphics of *Baby Boom* add to this minor-cinematic experience: pulsating between basic colors, explicitly in the stroboscopic "Disco" (100-109), where light as much as motion is the subject, an amp'd-up version of the warming flicker that pervades the whole book, which we are meant to sit back and read with Victorian delight, like born-again media consumers, turning the pages as one might the crank of a toy projector, enjoying these snippets stripped of narrative and offering paneled breakdowns as nothing more than a system for representing motion unfolding in time—a primitive form that modern comics historically never assumed, even in the highly chronographic examples by Willette and Steinlen, which are swabbed in story from the go. Or looking ahead, maybe *Baby Boom* is the proto-TikTok of comics.

The original version of this essay was published on the website *Comics Comics*, run by Dan Nadel and Tim Hodler, in July 2010. It has been overhauled for clarity, accuracy, tone, and the present.

rather than a single one treated at length, as in *Travel*. There are two pages on dam-building, sixteen on housecleaning, two on cooking, six on fishing, seven on using a hula hoop, one on origami, two about school, two about fieldtrips, and so on. It would be physically impossible for Yokoyama to create 200-page works on each of these topics, so *Baby Boom* offers a series of sketch digests instead.

There is also something early-cinema-like about *Baby Boom*, in that it recalls motifs and sensibilities of cinema as the medium came into being and first circulated publicly circa 1900. It is different from the references to lantern slides, zoopraxiscopes, and early animation that one finds in, say, the work of collector-creator Chris Ware, who remains deeply nostalgic even while pioneering new paths. It is also different from the "cinematic" as it is usually construed in comics, as an adaptation of montage and camera work.

At his first largescale museum exhibition, at the Kawasaki City Museum in 2010, Yokoyama summed up his practice as simply "I draw time," which I think means more than "I create manga that foreground the experience of temporal duration." Many of the intermedial references in his work—from picture books and encyclopedias in "Book" and *Garden*, to quasi-filmstrips and projectors in *Travel*, to photographers in *Travel* and *Garden*, to the library and giant map of *Garden*—feel as if they have been introduced to compensate for the fact that comics, as a medium of still sequential images, simply cannot capture duration fully, let alone reproduce it. Comics figure time selected and collected rather than experienced: "I draw ciphers of time," in other words. Up to *Baby Boom*, these temporal references were often comically grandiose, bubbling with the enthusiasm of a recent convert (Yokoyama began as a painter) who thinks that the object of his new faith can do anything, transcend its own limits, outstrip other media on their home turfs. The mega-landforms of *New Engineering* and the apocalypse that ends *Garden* are signs that all of this occurs under the figure of the sublime and a kind of Icarian hubris: the artist knows that they are attempting the impossible and there will be a fall.

With *Baby Boom*, Yokoyama sets aside these totalizing figures in favor of friendly, human-scaled fragments. This is where the diminutive, early-cinema quality comes in. I first felt this while reading what is otherwise one of the book's less notable episodes, "Vending Machine" (117). Chick and bird-father walk up to a vending machine. They insert money, push a button, receive their canned soft drink, share it, finish it, and chuck the empty can into a recycling bin. The warmth stems in part from the preciousness of parent and child sharing everyday life. But there is also something about this episode, and many others in *Baby Boom*, that reminds me of the early motion pictures of the Lumière brothers: where what was displayed was often banal, of mild or no interest if seen in real life (workers exiting the factory, a boat leaving harbor, a train arriving into station), but when projected serially offered a survey of everyday activities and non-events, the primary attraction of which was their presentation as cinematic events. This was, to use a popular term from film studies popularized by Tom Gunning, "a cinema of attractions" versus a later cinema that depended on plot and charismatic characters to enthrall audiences.

of melodrama, sweaty action, and bodily humor in most manga by men, his rejection of human psychology, emotions, and bodily sensation was indeed unique. He would continue in that vein with *World Map Room* (2013) and *Iceland* (2016), which he describes as mock hardboiled gekiga in the school of *Golgo 13*. *Baby Boom*, in contrast, is warm—warm as an incubator, let's say—and not just because of the electric colors.

Yokoyama refers to the smaller of the two main characters as a "bird chick" (*hiyoko*), though it looks to me more like a piece of lint with a face and limbs. He mentions the kids' shows *Anpanman* and *Hamtaro* as inspirations, but I also think of Q-Taro, the white waddling ghost by Fujiko Fujio, their precursor to Doraemon. This "chick" has a chaperon: the cone-faced character with the spherical head who appears in earlier works, referred to in the interview as a "birdman." Many of the episodes in *Baby Boom* show these two engaging in activities—eating, playing catch, fishing, cleaning house, going to an amusement park—that suggest not just a wholesome parent-child relationship, as Yokoyama says in the interview, but a father and son relationship specifically (in fact, the vast majority of Yokoyama's characters read to me as male), though this dad does way more around the house than most Japanese dads do. Joe Kessler mentioned to me that *Baby Boom* reminds him of E. O. Plauen's pantomime strip *Father and Son* (1934-37). I think that's a great comparison, even for its contrasts. The looser way Yokoyama constructs visual gags and punchlines (when he includes them at all) show him to be operating typically at a more immanent level.

When I first picked up *Baby Boom*, I figured Yokoyama recently had a kid, the change from his earlier work being so stark, and the depiction of parent-child care and play so happy. But no. The interview explains that this was the delayed result of being around children through a friend who was a parent and another who taught at a kindergarten. Yokoyama also talks, in the interview and elsewhere, about how the tourists in *Garden* are like kids: going where they please, doing what they please, innocently but ruinously. He compares *New Engineering* to kids playing with sand, blurting out GWEEEN (machinery moving) and DOKAAN (crashing) as they build and destroy. The obi (belly band) of the Japanese edition of *Baby Boom* even offers the following from Nietzsche's *Thus Spoke Zarathustra*: "Innocence is the child, and forgetfulness, a new beginning." Though not very Nietzschean in spirit, it was also around this time that Yokoyama started selling plush toys based on his characters. If I was ever appointed to curate a show of Yokoyama's work, I might simply title it *Kindergarten*, for what is his world but an oversized "children's garden"?

Baby Boom also elaborates, I think, on a less obvious theme running through Yokoyama's early work: fantasies of the book as a totalizing medium. This is clearest in *Garden*, with its Borgesian-like library of countless picture encyclopedias on endless shelves, and a giant map on the roof. I view *Travel* in an analogous way, as a kind of narrativized picture encyclopedia of all the things that could happen over the course of a single train ride. In *New Engineering*, likewise, a number of the flying folios in the chapter "Book" are encyclopedic in nature. Considering these precedents, *Baby Boom* might be seen as an index-like sampler of the fantasy picture library in *Garden*, presenting a range of activities each in condensed form

could be quite strong at first. With *Outdoors*, the eye no longer raced with the madness. You'd seen the art before. You knew its codes. You had come to understand what sorts of subject matter it's good for. The inventor was in need of reinvention.

Then came *Baby Boom*, originally serialized in the magazine *Web Designing* in 2008-09 and published as a book near the end of 2009 by East Press. While sporting many of the classic Yokoyama themes and graphic motifs, *Baby Boom* approaches them in a novel way. The artwork isn't black and white, for one. Drawn with magic markers, most of the 39 episodes (ranging from one to eighteen pages) are composed in two colors, rarely just one, sometimes three or four, or more. The polychromy is used to separate figures from background and/or sound effects, effects from background or each other, important details or objects from all of the above—or the inverse, to merge the otherwise distinct into common categories to confuse the eye. The technique electrifies the best episodes with a pulsating push-pull or flicker effect (there's even an episode of dancing under disco lights) that would be muddled by adding more colors or using color in a painterly manner. The most manic chapter, "Catch" (pages 88-95), shows the two stars of *Baby Boom* throwing a baseball back and forth for eight pages, at first carefully in the air, then faster, then some tricky grounders, before the ball sails over one of their heads and into a stream. As the game gets more intense and precarious, the staid red-blue of the beginning percolates into a purple-aquamarine red-olive kaleidoscope. I bet neon light artists would love *Baby Boom*.

The technique came out of the artist's own working process. I don't know if Yokoyama always did things this way, but at least for *Outdoors* he first sketched things out in color marker pens on standard copy paper, then cut apart the panels, reassembled them as he saw fit on a light box, and finally traced them in black on another sheet of paper. This I know from seeing a show of his underdrawings in January 2009 at the Aoyama Book Center in Tokyo. According to the interview included in the Japanese book edition of *Baby Boom* (translated herein), Yokoyama began what became *Baby Boom* in rough black marker versus his signature pseudo-mechanical precision. But his editors feared the product looked lazy, recommending neat color separation so that speed and looseness looked like a virtue. The deskilled aesthetic Yokoyama was toying with when he commenced *Baby Room* would find other outlets, however. It explodes in the oversize *Baby Boom Final* (2010), with its fragmented and painterly-markerly collages. It courts punky-junkiness in *Room* (2013), a self-described "gag manga" composed of crudely pasted-up sketches in monochrome. But also go back to *Travel*, to those late afternoon sun segments where the light casts sharp and quickly changing shadows upon the passengers... A desire for expressionistic facture had stirred in the heart of the geometer for years.

Another new thing about *Baby Boom* is its humanity. To be sure, Yokoyama's previous works have humans—or humanoids, as they are all fairly cold and stiff in their movements, speech, and physical look. They act like automatons as often as they do people. In interviews, Yokoyama has spoken distastefully of "the stink of humans." Given the pervasiveness

BABY BOOM AND THE COMICS OF ATTRACTION

RYAN HOLMBERG

Their differences notwithstanding, Yokoyama Yuichi's first three books take their readers on playfully dystopian journeys through landscapes developed for leisure tourism. In *New Engineering* (2004), open plots are invaded, filled, and ripped apart to create bizarre landforms and public works mainly for recreational use. In *Travel* (2006), three men ride in one of the icons of Japan as the technological and administrative master of frictionless flows and timetables—the high-speed Bullet Train—consuming landscape from the comfort of padded seats on their way to a seaside getaway, the imagery warping and fragmenting along the way. In *Garden* (2007), a phalanx of men traverses a modern sculpture park-cum-obstacle course, playing recklessly with its objects.

The comparison once made on the blog *Transatlantis* between Yokoyama's structures and Isamu Noguchi's posthumously finished Moerenuma Park in Sapporo, similarly equipped with man-made mini-mountains and cuboid "play sculptures" for clambering, feels spot on. *Takeshi's Castle* also comes to mind, with *Garden* at least. In general, I think it useful to think about Yokoyama's reworking of modernist avant-garde styles (like Futurism in *Travel*) and fantasy architecture (like Étienne-Louis Boullée's *Cenotaph to Newton* in *New Engineering*) through the lens of recreational play and tourism—the latter considering the recurring motifs of the sightseer and photographer. Obvious in *Travel*, this also applies to *Garden*, its trespassers the perfect image of the thoughtless tourist group, their activities causing the destruction of the consumed landscape, which blows apart in an apocalyptic hurricane at the manga's end. Throughout Yokoyama's work, you find classic modernist tropes—mass mobilization, advanced military, surveillance, and transportation technologies, visionary architecture, geometric abstraction, an obsession with speed and sensation—retooled for a leisure economy. It's a topical spin in post-industrial Japan, where efforts have been made to physically reshape the archipelago for a first class "leisure society" of parks, art, and resorts while farms, mines, and factories wither and die. Art historically, this puts Yokoyama's modernism closer to the Grosvenor School, with their dynamic but apolitical prints of people commuting and exercising, than to the original Italian Futurists or their British counterparts, the Vorticists.

With its campers, makeshift shelters, and real-life gamers, *Outdoors* (2009) was clearly an extension of his debut trilogy. But suddenly it felt like Yokoyama was working on auto. There were weird structures, again. Big sound effects, again. Men jumped around. Projectiles flew. With earlier works, the eye got trapped and strung in Yokoyama's nets of intersecting lines and layered sound effects. Eventually you'd find your bearings and be able to read through the story with fair ease, but the diverting force of abstraction

YY I originally planned to draw the whole thing in black and white, but the editor who oversaw its original serialization [in the magazine *Web Designing*] told me, "The drawing is loose, which looks sloppy coming from someone known for detailed drawing." So, our solution was to make the linework clearer by using different colors. It was at someone else's request, but I like how it turned out.

EP The drawing does have a rough touch.

YY It was supposed to be even rougher than this. Partly that was a reaction to drawing in detail for so many years. But I also thought that rough pictures might be more interesting, so I had the idea of exploiting the sketched touch of manga underdrawings.

EP There are panels like that inserted between the chapters of *New Engineering*, like intermissions.

YY That's right. There's nothing inherently wrong with coarse lines. But they can easily slip into looking messy. I want to improve my technique with that. I don't want to have to depend on neatness and prettiness, on the quality of handwork. I also want to get readers to engage more directly with the content of what's drawn.

EP Your past work is composed of sharp lines that almost look like they weren't made by hand.

YY That was also to drain the drawing of human bodily warmth, to block my own feelings from entering the drawing. But recently I realized that's possible even if the drawing is rough. Though I drew cute things in *Baby Boom*, I did so from a standpoint that's adequately detached, so there's no question of being sucked in by the cuteness.

EP Is that different than the emotional distance parents take with regards to their children?

YY I don't want to lose objectivity. When parents take photographs of their kids, if the child makes a strange face the parents will usually want to delete that shot. I have a friend who likes those kind of photos and does the opposite. "Look at how funny my kid looks!" they'll say, showing me the photo. Seeing your own supposedly cute kid as also comical is closer to my stance.

EP Will you not make neatly drawn works like you used to anymore?

YY I have no intention of stopping making the kind of work I have been. I still have a number of manga that I want to draw that require detailed drawing in pen. All problems require their own solutions.

The Japanese version of this interview accompanied the original book edition of *Baby Boom* (Tokyo: East Press, 2009). It has been slightly shortened for content.

toward it, not caring about anybody else, to the point where they even climb over one another. That's cute. There's plenty of food, but they still scramble for every last morsel.

EP You think, "How stupid!"

YY Yes, it's stupid. It's stupid in the way the manga I've drawn with sharp pen lines are stupid. Like *Garden* (2007), where everyone crowds around and gawks at these weird objects, working hard to build these things that seem to have no meaning. It is very stupid.

EP Even though it's drawn neatly.

YY *Garden* begins with people trespassing through a wall. It's the kind of stupid thing that elementary schoolers would do.

EP In *New Engineering* (2004), there are lots of odd but simple sound effects, like the primitive noises kids make when they're absorbed in make-believe.

YY They'll go like GWEEEN and DOKAAN while building and destroying mounds in the sand. They often imagine those sounds in their head, then sometimes make them out loud.

EP Sorry if this comes across as rude, but would you describe yourself as also having those childish qualities?

YY Absolutely. Everyone in *Garden* is essentially me. However, those early works are primarily about the passage of time. Comedy and cuteness are there only as supplements. *Baby Boom* (2009), on the other hand, is about looking at movement and experiencing its cuteness. I put my heart and soul into trying to draw the chick's face as cute as I could. I don't know how many times I redrew it to get it right. Bird chicks are basically expressionless, so I wanted to capture that too.

EP They definitely have an empty, oblivious look. So, the round character in the manga is a chick, and this bird-like human is an adult bird?

YY That's right.

EP The birdmen in your previous manga were human, so I assumed that was the case this time too. But here it's actually a bird.

YY They could be human. It doesn't really matter. Together those two characters are meant to symbolize parent and child, or big and small, or older and younger. I'd rather not fix their identity. It doesn't matter to me which is the parent and which is the kid, what their names are or where they live, or anything like that.

EP So, the chick could be the adult.

YY That's a possibility. Look at this page (83). The chick's the one driving and the other one's lost their cool.

EP Why did you draw *Baby Boom* in color?

YOKOYAMA YUICHI
QUERIED BY EAST PRESS

EP *Baby Boom* is quite different in style from your previous work. I imagine it might throw your readers a bit. Why the change?

YY About fifteen years ago, I started finding cute things interesting. I spent a lot of time with my friend's kid. I also had the opportunity to be around children a lot through an acquaintance who worked at a kindergarten. That's when I realized how comical kids can be. For example, there's this TV program for little kids called *Together with Mom* (*Okaasan to issho*). The young guy in charge will say, "Okay, now go like this!" and do an action for viewers to mimic. But you'll have one kid just staring off into space, with a clump of food sitting in their mouth, without chewing or spitting it out, until finally their parent runs over and pulls it out. Or another kid will fall hard on their face, then stand right back up without flinching or crying, like nothing happened. I started thinking about the comical nature of those kind of things.

EP Do you think there's a connection between that kind of comicality and cuteness?

YY Yes. It helped me see the comical side of adults, too, and from there of all living creatures. People laugh when they watch shows about cute baby animals, or when they look at photobooks about dwarf rabbits or ferrets or Pomeranians. It's that unconscious behavior of little animals.

EP The animals don't pay attention to what's going on around them, they don't care.

YY For years, I wanted to draw that, but only now have I figured out how. The solution lay in babifying the kind of characters I'd been drawing. Initially I wanted to draw something like *Anpanman*, with a world with all sorts of grand characters whirling around. But that turned out to be too much work technically. But with something like the Ham-Hams kingdom in the *Trotting Hamtaro* (*Tottoko Hamutaro*) movies, there's all these hamsters that look similar but are different colors, right?

EP Is that so?

YY You've never seen them? A few years ago, I watched all the *Hamtaro* videos in one go. When it comes to comedy, you've got to see them. The creators, I am sure, knew exactly what they were doing. As a different example, look at animals when they're being totally selfish, like when a food tray is put out and they all scurry

Baby Boom
Yokoyama Yuichi

English edition published
in 2022 by Breakdown Press,
London, UK

Designed by Jean-Philippe Bretin

Manga SFX Translated by Céline Bruel & Ryan Holmberg

Colour Separations by Éditions Matière

Art Direction by Joe Kessler

Print Production by Joe Hales studio

English language edition
licensed through East Press, Tokyo

ISBN: 978-1-911081-19-7

First editi[illegible]

Breakdown Press
1 Berwick Street
London W1F 0DR

www.breakdownpress.com

FOR THE MANGA BEGIN AT THE OTHER SIDE OF THIS BOOK AND READ PANELS

TO LEFT